About the Author

Günter Grass, who achieved lasting international fame with his first novel, *The Tin Drum*, regarded as the quintessential post-Second World War novel, is a creative artist of stunning versatility: novelist, poet, dramatist, and graphic artist who designs his own jackets and produces a running commentary in drawings and etchings on his literary work. He is also a Social Democrat actively involved in electoral politics, and a rousing speaker. Among his many works are the novels *Dog Years*, *Local Anaesthetic*, *From the Diary of a Snail*, *The Flounder*, the novella *Cat and Mouse*, and various collections of poems, plays, and political speeches.

Günter Grass

The Meeting at Telgte

Translated by Ralph Manheim

Afterword by Leonard Forster

FAWCETT CREST • NEW YORK

THE MEETING AT TELGTE

THIS BOOK CONTAINS THE COMPLETE TEXT OF THE ORIGINAL HARDCOVER EDITION.

Published by Fawcett Crest Books, CBS Educational and Professional Publishing, a division of CBS Inc., by arrangement with Harcourt Brace Jovanovich, Inc.

ISBN: 0-449-24504-7

Printed in the United States of America

First Fawcett Crest Printing: May 1982

10 9 8 7 6 5 4 3 2 1

Publisher's Note

The historical background to the events and personalities dealt with in this novel may be unfamiliar to English and American readers. Leonard Forster has provided an afterword and notes on the dramatis personae (pp. 200–220) identifying the historical, literary, and commercial streams that had their confluence at Telgte.

1

The thing that hath been tomorrow is that which shall be yesterday. Our stories of today need not have taken place in the present. This one began more than three hundred years ago. So did many other stories. Every story set in Germany goes back that far. If I am writing down what happened in Telgte, it is because a friend, who gathered his fellow writers around him in the forty-seventh year of our century, is soon to celebrate his seventieth birthday; and yet he is older, much older than that—and we, his present-day friends, have all grown hoary white with him since those olden times.

Up from Jutland and down from Regensburg came Lauremberg and Greflinger on foot; others came on horseback or in covered wagons. While some were sailing down rivers, old

Weckherlin took ship from London to Bremen. From far and near they came, from all directions. A merchant, to whom due dates mean profit and loss, might well have been amazed at the punctual zeal displayed by those men of mere verbal action, especially at a time when the towns and countryside were still, or once again, ravaged, overgrown with nettles and thistles, depopulated by plague, and when all the roads were unsafe.

So much so that Moscherosch and Schneuber, who had come from Strassburg, reached their appointed destination stripped of everything they owned (except their portfolios, useless to highwaymen), Moscherosch laughing and richer by a satire, Schneuber lamenting and already dreading the horrors of the return journey. (His arse was sore from blows with the flat of the sword.)

Only because Czepko, Logau, Hofmannswaldau, and other Silesians, provided with a safe-conduct issued by Wrangel, had attached themselves to various Swedish battalions, whose foraging raids took them as far as Westphalia, were they able to reach Osnabrück undiminished; but they suffered as if in their own flesh from the daily atrocities of the foraging parties, who showed no concern for any poor devil's religion. No remonstrances would hold Wrangel's horsemen in check. The student Scheffler (a discovery of Czepko's) was almost done in while trying to shield a peasant woman who, like her husband before her, was to be impaled before the eyes of her children.

Johann Rist came via Hamburg from nearby Wedel on the Elbe. A coach had brought Mülbe, the Strassburg publisher, from Lüneburg. The route taken by Simon Dach, whose invitations had provoked all this effort, from the Kneiphof section of Königsberg, was indeed the longest, but also the safest, for he had traveled in the retinue of Frederick William, Elector of Brandenburg. The previous year Frederick William had become engaged to Louise of Orange, and Dach had been privileged to recite his panegyric verses in Amsterdam. It was then that the many letters of invitation, complete with designation of the meeting place, were written, and that, with the elector's help, provision was made for their delivery. (The elector's ubiquitous political agents were often required to double as couriers.) This was how Gryphius received his invitation, though he had been traveling for the past year with the Stettin merchant Wilhelm Schlegel, first in Italy, then in France, and Dach's letter was delivered to him on his return journey (in Speyer, to be exact). He set out at once and brought Schlegel with him.

Augustus Buchner, magister of letters, arrived punctually from Wittenberg. After declining several times, Paul Gerhardt nevertheless arrived on time. Philipp Zesen, whose letter caught up with him in Hamburg, traveled from Amsterdam with his publisher. No one wanted to miss the meeting. Nothing, no school, state, or court function, could keep them away. Those who lacked funds for the journey went looking for patrons. Those who, like Greflinger, had found no patron were carried to their destination by obstinacy. And those whose obstinacy might have deterred them from starting in time were infected with travel fever by the news that others were already on their way. Even such men as Zesen and Rist, who counted each other as enemies, were intent on meeting. Logau's curiosity about the meeting proved even stronger than his scorn for the assembled poets. Their local surroundings were too constricting. No business transaction, however intricate, no love affair, however diverting, could resist the force that drew them together. Moreover, the peace negotiations brought increasing unrest. No one wanted to be by himself.

But eagerly as the gentlemen had responded to Dach's invitation in their hunger for literary exchange, they soon lost heart when they failed to find quarters in Oesede, the village near Osnabrück where the meeting was to be held. Though reservations had been made in plenty of time, the Black Horse, where the conferees were to have lodged, had been commandeered by the staff of Swedish War Councilor Erskein, who had recently put the demands of Wrangel's armies for indemnification before the peace conference, so adding appreciably to the cost of the peace. What rooms were not occupied by regimental secretaries and colonels in Count Königsmark's army were piled high with documents. The great hall, where they planned to meet, to carry on the discussions for which they had so fervently longed and to read their manuscripts to one another, had been turned into a storeroom. Everywhere horsemen and musketeers were lounging about. Couriers came and went. Erskein made himself inaccessible. A provost, to whom Dach presented a document showing that he had rented the Black Horse, was seized with a fit of circumfluously infectious laughter when Dach requested that his down payment be reimbursed by the Swedes. Brusquely rebuffed, Dach came back. Strong, stupid men. Their armored emptiness. Their grinning dullness. None of the Swedish officers had ever heard of the illustrious visitors. Grudgingly, they let them rest a while in the taproom. The landlord advised them to move on to the Oldenburg region, where everything, even lodging, was available.

Already the Silesians were thinking of going on to Hamburg, Gerhardt of returning to Berlin, Moscherosch and Schneuber of proceeding to Holstein with Rist; already Weckherlin had decided to take the next ship to London; already most of the travelers, not without recriminations against Dach, were threatening to let the meeting go hang, and already Dach—ordinarily the soul of equanimity—was beginning to have doubts about his plan; already they were standing in the street with their luggage, uncertain

which way to turn, when—well before nightfall—
the Nuremberg contingent arrived; Harsdörffer
with his publisher Endter, and young Birken;
they were accompanied by a red-bearded fellow
who called himself Christoffel Gelnhausen and
whose gangling youthfulness—he seemed to be
in his middle twenties—was contradicted by his
pockmarked face. In his green doublet and
plumed hat he looked like something out of a
storybook. Someone said that he had been begotten by Count Mansfeld's soldiery on their way
through—but Gelnhausen turned out to be
more real than he looked. He was in command
of a detachment of imperial horsemen and musketeers, who were camped at the edge of town
because the territory of the towns where the
peace conference was being held had been
declared neutral ground, barred to the military
action of both parties.

When Dach had described the poets' sorry
situation to the Nurembergers, and Gelnhausen
had offered his services in a long-winded speech
well larded with tropes, Harsdörffer took Dach
aside. True, he said, the fellow prates like an
itinerant astrologer—he had introduced himself to the assemblage as Jupiter's favorite,
whom, as they could see, Venus had punished
in France— but he had wit, and was better read
than his clowning might lead one to suspect.
Moreover, he was serving as a secretary at the
headquarters of the Schauenburg regiment, then
stationed in Offenburg. In Cologne, where the

12

Nurembergers had arrived by ship from Würzburg, Gelnhausen had helped them out of difficulties incurred when Endter had attempted to sell a stack of books without a license. Fortunately Gelnhausen had been able to talk them clear of clerical suspicion, which scented "heretical machinations." His lies, said Harsdörffer, are as inspired as any romances; his eloquence reduces the very Jesuits to silence; not just the church fathers, but all the gods and their planets are at his fingertips; he is familiar with the seamy side of life, and wherever he goes, in Cologne, in Recklinghausen, in Soest, he knows his way about. Quite possibly, Harsdörffer concluded, he might help them.

Gerhardt warned them against dealing with a man of the imperial party. Hofmannswaldau stood dumbfounded; hadn't the fellow just quoted a passage from Opitz's translation of the *Arcadia*? Moscherosch and Rist thought they should listen at least to the regimental secretary's proposals, especially after Schneuber of Strassburg had asked him about certain particulars of life in the bustling garrison town of Offenburg and received bathhouse gossip in reply.

In the end, Gelnhausen was given leave to explain himself to the assembled and now desperately unquartered gentlemen. His words seemed as trustworthy as the sheen of the double row of buttons on his green doublet. Being a cousin of Mercury and therefore as restlessly active as that god, he was, so he averred, bound

13

for Münster in any case—at the bidding of his master, an acolyte of Mars, in other words a colonel—carrying a secret message to Count Trauttmannsdorff, who, in his capacity as head of the emperor's negotiating team, had been crammed full of wisdom by the peevish Saturn—in order that peace might dawn at last. The trip came to less than thirty miles. Under an almost full moon. And through flat country. And if their lordships decided to avoid priest-ridden Münster, they would pass through Telgte, a snug little town which, though impoverished, had remained unscarred, since the townspeople had managed to beat off the Hessians and had not wearied of feeding the Königsmark regimental treasury. And since, as they must know, Telgte had long been a place of pilgrimage, there he would find quarters for their lordships, those pilgrims of the Muses. For he learned early on to find lodging for all manner of gods.

When old Weckherlin asked what they, as Protestants, had done to deserve so much Catholic favor (after all, Gelnhausen was bearing swift tidings to the Catholic party), the regimental secretary replied that he cared little for religion, as long as no one interfered with his own. And that his message for Trauttmannsdorff was not so secret as all that, since everyone knew that the Saxon regiments in Marshal Turenne's camp had mutinied against their foreign overlords and dispersed. Such news ran on ahead, so there was no point in hurrying. He

14

therefore preferred to oblige a dozen homeless poets, all the more so since he himself—by Apollo!—wielded the pen, though for the present only in Colonel Schauenburg's regimental chancellery.

At that Dach accepted his offer. Whereupon Gelnhausen stopped talking tortuous foolishness and issued orders to his horsemen and musketeers.

2

Since the start of the peace negotiations, which by then had been in progress for almost three years, the road from Osnabrück via Telgte to Münster had been much traveled in both directions, from the Protestant to the Catholic camp and contrariwise, by couriers in carriages and on horseback, bearing an archive-glutting mass of petitions, memoranda, scheming missives, invitations to festivities, and agents' reports on the latest military movements, which had been going on undeterred by the peace negotiations. The military lineup of the contending parties was not determined by religious allegiance: Catholic France, with papal approval, had fought against Spain, the Habsburgs, and Bavaria; the Protestant Saxons sometimes had one and some-times the other foot in the imperial camp; a few years earlier, the Lutheran Swedes had attacked the Lutheran Danes. In deep secret Bavaria was bargaining for possession of the Palatinate. Other factors were armies that had mutinied or changed sides, internal conflicts in the Netherlands, the eternal lamentations of the Silesian Estates, the impotence of the imperial cities, the changing but not diminishing land hunger of the allies, in consequence of which, when the conference agreed the year before that Alsace should be ceded to France and Pomerania to Sweden, the delegates from Strassburg and the Baltic towns ran themselves and their horses ragged (in vain) on the road between Osnabrück and Münster. Which was not to be surprised at, for the state of the roads to and from the conference towns was equaled only by the state of the negotiations and of Germany itself.

In any event, though Gelnhausen borrowed, or, rather, requisitioned, four wagons in next to no time, they took longer than expected to convey the homeless gentlemen—more than twenty in number—from the foothills of Teutoburg Forest through the Tecklenburg plain to Telgte. (The sacristan's offer to provide temporary quarters in an empty convent near Oesede, where the Swedes had lodged, was declined, for the devastated building was lacking in the slightest comfort; only Logau and Czepko, who distrusted Gelnhausen, spoke in favor of accepting.)

The colors of the summer evening were fading behind them when Simon Dach paid the bridge toll for his party. And immediately after the bridge across the outer Ems, but before the inner arm of the river, which bounds the city on the Ems Gate side, Gelnhausen, in his own characteristic way, billeted the company at the Bridge Tavern, a thatch-roofed, tall-gabled stone structure planted in the middle of the otherwise unoccupied water meadows and at first sight showing little war damage. Taking aside the landlady, with whom he was evidently acquainted, he exchanged whispers with her and then introduced her to Dach, Rist, and Harsdörffer as Libuschka, a friend of long years' standing. An aging woman under a layer of face paint, she was wrapped in a horse blanket and wore soldier's breeches, but spoke with refinement and claimed descent from the Bohemian nobility. From the very start, she said, her father had fought for the Protestant cause with Bethlen Gabor. Cognizant of the honor being shown her house, she promised to provide the company with lodging, perhaps not at once, but very shortly.

Thereupon Gelnhausen and his imperial troops created such a hubbub outside the stables, in front of the tavern, in the front hall, on the stairs, and outside all the rooms that the chained dogs came close to choking. They didn't stop until all the guests and their coachmen had been jolted out of their sleep. No sooner had the gentlemen—they were Hanseatic merchants come from Lemgo, on their way to Bremen—gathered in front of the Bridge Tavern than

Gelnhausen commanded them to leave the house forthwith. And he backed up his order by informing them that all who loved their lives should keep their distance, since several of the listless, wasted figures in and around the wagons had been stricken with the plague and were candidates for the charnel house. He and his detachment, he explained, were escorting a group of unfortunates whom it was necessary to remove, lest their presence incommode the peace negotiations, for which reason he, body physician to Signor Chigi, the papal nuncio, had not only imperial, but Swedish orders as well, to convey the diseased persons to quarantine. He therefore bade the merchants leave immediately and without argument, barring which he would be obliged to burn their vehicles and wares on the riverbank. The plague—as everyone knew and as he, a physician endowed with all the wisdom of Saturn, could assure them—was no respecter of wealth, but on the contrary delighted in ravishing treasures and took special pleasure in searing gentlemen in Brabant cloth with its torrid breath.

When the merchants asked for a written statement justifying their eviction, Gelnhausen drew his sword, called it his goose quill, asked to whom his first missive should be addressed, and added that in the name of the emperor and his adversaries he must urgently—by Mars and his ferocious dogs!—request the departing guests of the Bridge Tavern to observe the strictest silence concerning the reason for their sudden departure.

After this address, the inn was quickly evacuated. Carriages had never been harnessed more briskly. If anyone hesitated, the musketeers sprang to his help. Before Dach and several of the poets could protest loudly enough the immorality of Gelnhausen's trick, the house had been taken over. With misgivings, to be sure, but reassured by Moscherosch and Greflinger, who took the proceedings as a farce deserving to be laughed at, the poets repaired to the evacuated rooms and still-warm beds.

Since in addition to the merchant Schlegel, several printers from Strassburg, Amsterdam, Hamburg, and Breslau had, in their capacity as publishers, accepted Dach's invitation, the landlady Libuschka was easily compensated for her loss, especially because the evicted Hanseatics had left several bolts of cloth and a few pieces of silverware behind them, not to mention four kegs of Rhenish brown beer.

Gelnhausen's soldiers made themselves at home in the stables that were built onto one side of the house. From the entrance hall, between the taproom and the kitchen (to which the great hall was attached), the poets climbed two flights of stairs to the top floor of the Bridge Tavern. Already they were easier in their minds. Only the choice of rooms permitted of some friction. Zesen quarreled with Lauremberg after having had words with Rist. The medical student Scheffler was in tears. Since there were not enough rooms, Dach bedded him, Birken, and Greflinger in the attic straw.

At that point it became known that old Weckherlin's pulse was failing. Schneuber, who shared a room with Moscherosch, demanded ointment for his wounds. Gerhardt and Magister Buchner both wanted rooms to themselves. Hofmannswaldau doubled up with Gryphius, Czepko with Logau. Harsdörffer kept close to Endter, his publisher. Rist was drawn to Zesen and Zesen to Rist. In all this the landlady and her maids lent the new guests a helping hand. Libuschka was familiar with some of the gentlemen's names. She was able to recite several stanzas of Gerhardt's hymns. She gratified Harsdörffer with elegant quotations from his *Garden of the Pegnitz Pastoral*. And, later, sitting in the taproom with Moscherosch and Lauremberg—who had no desire for bed but preferred to stay up until morning over brown beer, bread, and cheese—she was able, in succinct sentences, to sum up several of the dream visions from Moscherosch's *Philander*. She might have been made to order for a meeting of poets, so well read was landlady Libuschka—or Courage, as she was called by Gelnhausen, who joined them after a while and was toasted for his prowess as a billeting officer.

Simon Dach also stayed awake. He lay in his room and once again mentally enumerated those he had summoned in letters, persuaded en route, forgotten intentionally or unintentionally, included in his list on someone's recommendation, or rejected, as well as those who had not yet arrived, among them his friend Albert, for whom the second bed in his room stood ready.

Sleep-banishing, sleepy-making worries: Maybe Schottel would come after all. (But the man from Wolfenbüttel stayed away, because Buchner had been invited.) The Nuremberg party made excuses for Klaj's absence on grounds of illness. Heaven help us if Rompler should come after all. Could Prince Ludwig reasonably be expected? (But the head of the Fruit-bearing Society remained in Köthen, offended: the prince detested Dach, who did not belong to the Order of the Palm Tree and made no bones about being a commoner.)

How fortunate that they had left word at the Black Horse in Oesede, saying where they would meet, in a different town but for the same reasons, namely, to rescue their cruelly maltreated language and to be near the peace negotiations. There they would sit until everything, the distress of the fatherland as well as the splendor and misery of poetry, had been discussed.

Opitz and Fleming would be missed. Would it be possible to keep theorizing to a minimum? Would anyone else turn up uninvited? Pondering these questions and physically longing for his wife, Regina, Dach slipped into sleep.

3

Or perhaps before retiring he wrote a letter to his Regina, née Pohl, who everywhere—in the Kneiphof quarter of Königsberg, by the students at the academy, among Dach's friends Albert, Blum, and Roberthin, and even by the elector—was referred to as Dach's Pohlin.* His letter started on a note of despair, then veered to amusement at the peripeties of the hunt for lodgings, and ended by commending the proceedings of the meeting to God's wisdom and mercy. Without delving into the deeper meaning of events, it merely recorded: how brutally the Swedes had expelled them from Oesede; how Gelnhausen, commonly referred to as Christoffel or Stoffel, had requisitioned four

*Pohlin, which is the feminine form of Pohl, sounds the same as *Polin*, Polish woman.—TRANS.

harnessed covered wagons from the carriage pool of the Protestant Estates; how at night, under a waxing moon, spared by the storms that were rumbling in the distance, they had followed the pitch torches of the imperial horsemen down the rutted Münster road as far as Telgte; how while still on the road Moscherosch, Greflinger, and Lauremberg had started swilling brandy, bellowing street songs, and teasing the always dignified Gerhardt; how Czepko and old Weckherlin had boldly leapt to the defense of the sensitive Gerhardt, with the result that, at least in three of the four wagons, hymns had been sung the rest of the way, and Gerhardt's recently published "Now hushed are woods and waters, At rest toil's sons and daughters, The world aslumber lies" had infected even the topers; and how nearly the whole company, including Gryphius (who had been sitting beside Dach and had grown fat all over), had fallen asleep while singing, so that no one had had time to reflect on Gelnhausen's outrageous trick of talking their company sick with plague so eloquently that the effluvia might have been smelled, until the end of the journey, when it was too late; and how despite or because of the damnable yet amusing (and he himself chose to be amused) immorality of the thing, they had all finally gone to bed, some laughing at the terrified haste of the fleeing moneybags and still drinking to the cruel joke, others quietly praying God for forgiveness, but all too tired to permit of any quarrels among the Silesians,

Nurembergers, and Strassburgers, which might have imperiled the meeting. Only between Rist and Zesen had there been flashes, as expected. On the other hand, since Schottel was not coming, Buchner promised to observe moderation. The Silesians, Dach's letter went on, had brought a frightened student with them; Hofmannswaldau wasn't acting at all like a scion of the nobility; all except Rist, who could not refrain from preaching, and Gerhardt, who was a stranger to literary life, were friendly to one another; even that whoremaster Greflinger was accommodating and had sworn by the infidelity of his Flora to behave with reasonable propriety; at the most, treachery might be expected of Schneuber, whom he, Dach, mistrusted. But if need be, he would know how to hold the company in check. Apart from the boozers in the taproom and himself, who was thinking of his Regina, only the double imperial guard that Gelnhausen had drawn up outside the Bridge Tavern for their protection were still awake. The landlady, though undoubtedly a trollop, was nevertheless an extraordinary woman, speaking fluent Italian with Gryphius, even standing up to Magister Buchner in Latin, and as thoroughly at home in the world of letters as a fox in a goose pen. Thus everything was turning out amazingly well, as though pursuant to a higher plan. The one thing that made him uneasy was the popish surroundings. Rumor had it that secret meetings of Anabaptists were being held in Telgte. The ghost of Knipperdolling still haunted the place. A spooky sort of town, but clearly suitable for a congress.

What more Simon Dach wrote to his Regina I shall leave to the two of them. Only his last, sleep-bringing thoughts are still within my reach: they circled around pros and cons, lagged behind and ran ahead of events, made various persons enter and exit, repeated themselves. I shall put them in order.

Dach had no doubts about the utility of the meeting that had been so long in preparation. As long as the war was going on, meetings had been more longed for than planned. Opitz, for instance, contemplating such a gathering only a short while before his death, had written from his haven in Danzig: "A meeting of all possible poets should be held in Breslau or in Prussia, to unite our confraternity in these days of the fatherland's division. . . ."

But no one, not even Opitz, would have been so acceptable to the dispersed writers as Dach, whose wide-ranging mind and generously dispensed warmth made for a gathering of sufficient scope to encompass a lone vagrant like Greflinger, an aristocratic aesthete like Hofmannswaldau, and the unliterary Gerhardt, but who nevertheless imposed restrictions, for no invitations were sent to the poetasters who toadied to princely patrons and were interested only in turning out encomiums and precommissioned elegies. Dach had gone so far as to ask his own prince, who could recite several of Dach's poems by heart and had contributed to the general travel fund, to remain benevolently absent.

Though certain members of the company (among them Buchner and Hofmannswaldau) had advised Dach to wait for the conclusion of the peace treaty or to hold the meeting at a distance from the war that was still raging—possibly in Polish Lissa or in unscarred Switzerland; though Zesen and the German-minded Association, which he had founded in Hamburg in the early forties, wished, in competition with Dach and in collaboration with Rompler's Upright Society of the Pine Tree, to organize a counter-meeting—Dach's persistence and political firmness had proved decisive. As a young man (under Opitz's influence), he had corresponded with Grotius, Bernegger, and the Heidelberg group around Lingelsheim, and consequently, though not active in diplomacy, as Opitz and Weckherlin still were at the time, he had regarded himself as an irenicist, a man of peace, ever since. In spite of Zesen, who backed down, and in opposition to the intrigues of the Strassburg magister Rompler, who was not invited, Simon Dach won out: it was arranged that in the forty-seventh year of the century (after twenty-nine years of war, the peace negotiations had not yet been concluded), a meeting should be held somewhere between Münster and Osnabrück, for the purpose of giving new force to the last remaining bond between all Germans, namely, the German language they held in common, and—if only from the side-lines—uttering a political word or two.

After all, they were not nobodies. Everything had been laid waste, words alone kept their luster. And where princes had disgraced themselves, poets had earned respect. They, not the powerful, were assured of immortality.

In any event Simon Dach was convinced that the meeting, if not he himself, was important. For—on a small scale and far from shot and shell, as they said in Königsberg—he had gathered poets and friends of the arts around him. Not only on Magistergasse, where thanks to a Kneiphof ordinance he enjoyed lifelong residence privileges, but also in the garden of Heinrich Albert the cathedral organist, on Lomse Island in the river Pregel, friends had met to read one another poems, most of which had been commissioned or written to celebrate one occasion or another: the usual poems and songs in honor of some marriage, which Albert would set to music. In jest the friends called themselves the Cucumber Lodge Society, knowing that side by side with other associations, such as the Fruit-bearing Order of the Palm Tree or the Strassburg Upright Society of the Pine Tree, or even with the Pegnitz Shepherds of Nuremberg, they were merely one branch of far-flung German poesy.

Early that afternoon, when the gentlemen had slept their fill, or slept off their drink, and had gathered in the great hall, Dach, knowing how eager they were to hear the whole tree murmur and feeling that a pun on his name was in order, made the following introductory remarks, proceeding after his fashion to speak now gaily, now gravely: "Let us, dear friends, foregather in my name—for it is I who invited you—as under one roof,* to the end that each of us may contribute according to his powers and through the resulting harmony establish a German-minded Pegnitz, Fruit-bearing, Upright Cucumber Lodge and Pine Tree Associations, and that in the forty-seventh year of this woeful century, our hitherto drowned-out voice be heard above all the long-winded talk of peace and despite the continuing clamor of battle; for what we have to say is not foreign-contaminated chatter, but part and parcel of our language: Where, O Germany, shall I leave you? For well nigh thirty years, by murder and rapine, Thou hast destroyed thyself, the guilt is thine. . . ."

*_Dach_ = roof.—TRANS.

4

Dach took these lines from his recently completed but not yet published poem lamenting the destruction of the cucumber bower on Lomse Island, which had been the meeting place of the Königsberg poets and had been sacrificed to the construction of a highway. Albert the cathedral organist had composed a three-part song in its memory.

Since Dach's lines aroused attention, Hofmannswaldau, Rist, Czepko, and others urged the author to recite the whole lament, which he did only later, on the third day, for he did not wish to open the meeting with his own production. Nor did he allow any further introductory speeches. (Zesen intended to say something fundamental about his German-minded Association and its division into guilds. Rist would have counterattacked, for he was already gestating the Order of Elbe Swans, which he was subsequently to found.)

Instead, Simon Dach, hoping to bring the company to look on Gerhardt as somewhat less of a stranger, asked him to say a prayer for the success of the meeting. Gerhardt stood up to do so, with Old Lutheran gravity and not without threatening with damnation the false prophets present; he must have had in mind the Silesian mystics or the Calvinists, if any.

Curtailing the silence that followed the prayer, Dach summoned his "most honored friends" to give a thought to those poets whose place would have been there among them had death not ravished them. All rose to their feet as he solemnly listed "those who too soon departed from us," naming first Opitz, then Fleming, then the political mentor of his generation, the irenicist Lingelsheim, then Zincgref; and finally he startled the assembly—Gryphius's countenance was clouded with displeasure—by evoking the memory of the Jesuit Spee von Langenfeld.

True, many of those present were acquainted with (and had indeed been influenced by) the much imitated Jesuit theater, and in his student days Gryphius had seen fit to translate several of the Jesuit Jakob Balde's Latin odes into German; true, Gelnhausen, whom no one outside of Harsdörffer (and Greflinger) regarded as a member of the assembly, had represented himself as a Catholic without giving anyone umbrage—but the posthumous honoring of Spee struck several of the Protestant gentlemen as going too far, even though they had accepted Dach's recommendation of tolerance. It would have provoked a loud protest or a wave of silent disgruntlement if Hofmannswaldau had not come to the help of Dach, who was trying, with a stern frown, to quell the general agitation by first quoting the "Penitential Hymn of a Contrite Heart" from Spee's anthology, *The Nightingale's Rival,* which had not yet been published, but copies of which were in circulation—"At nightfall when the darkness Clothes us black in shadow"—and then, as fluently as though he had carried the Latin original engraved in his mind, paraphrasing several passages from the *Cautio Criminalis,* Spee's indictment of the Inquisition and of torture. He then proceeded to laud the Jesuit's courage and (looking Gryphius straight in the eye) reminded his audience of how in blackest Würzburg Spee had seen some two hundred pitiful women subjected to torture; how when, maddened by pain, they had confessed, he had comforted them on their way to the stake; and finally of how, after committing his cruel experience to writing, he had published his eyewitness report as an indictment. And Hofmannswaldau concluded with the challenge: "Who among you can boast such courage?"

No answer was possible. Old Weckherlin was in tears. As though to add meaning, the student Scheffler said that Spee, like Opitz, had been carried off by the plague. Dach only made a note of the name and then handed Logau a printed text, wishing him—since all the dead were to be remembered—to read one of the sonnets that Fleming, who had died soon after Opitz, had written (while traveling in Nogaian Tartary) in his honor. And Logau also read his own elegy on the "Bober Swan,"* as Opitz was occasionally called: "In Latin there are many poets, Virgil is the greatest one. Likewise, among German singers, Opitz stands alone."

After honoring Lingelsheim, the friend of peace, Dach, in memory of Zincgref, read two selections from his book of precepts—light anecdotes that would relieve the tension—and, when he had finished, read one more on request.

Thus strained solemnity eased into amicable exchanges. Especially the older men knew stories about the departed. Weckherlin spoke of the young Opitz's doings in Heidelberg, in the days of the late lamented Lingelsheim. Buchner knew exactly what Fleming would have written if his Baltic Elsabe had not been unfaithful to him. The question was raised: why had Spee's poems thus far found no publisher? Then there was talk of student years in Leiden: Gryphius and Hofmannswaldau, Zesen and young Scheffler had been fed wild visionary ideas there. Someone (I?) asked why, in honoring the dead, Dach had neglected to mention the "Görlitz shoemaker," since after all the followers of Böhme were here represented.

In the meantime the landlady and her maids

*Opitz was ennobled as Opitz von Boberfeld. The Bober is a river on which his native town is situated.—TRANS.

had served a rather modest collation in the taproom. Dumplings floated in a soup fat with sausage broth. Flatbread was broken. Brown beer was on hand. You broke off a chunk, you dipped, you slobbered, you dipped again. Laughter went round and round. (What was the right way to pronounce this town on the Ems? Telgte or Telchte, or should one go so far as to say Tächte like the native maids?) Dach passed alongside the table, saying a few words to each man, and reconciling those who like Buchner and young Birken were becoming embroiled in argument ahead of time.

A discussion of the language was scheduled for after the meal. What had wrecked it, and what might make it well again? What rules should be laid down, and what rules would hamper the poetic flow? How might the so-called natural language, which Buchner disparaged as a "purely mystical concept," be nurtured with better fare and so develop into a national language? What should pass as High German and what place should be allotted to the dialects? For learned and polyglot as they all were—Gryphius and Hofmannswaldau were eloquent in seven tongues—they all mouthed and whispered, babbled and bellowed, declaimed and postured, in some sort of regional German.

Though he had been living and teaching mathematics in Danish Zeeland ever since Wallenstein's invasion of Pomerania, Lauremberg expressed himself in his native Rostock brogue, and Rist the Holstein preacher answered him in Low German. After thirty years of residence in London, the diplomat Weckherlin still spoke an unvarnished Swabian. And into the predominantly Silesian conversation, Moscherosch mixed his Alemannic, Harsdörffer his peppery Franconian, Buchner and Gerhardt their Saxon, Greflinger his Lower Bavarian gargle, and Dach a Prussian kneaded and shaped between Memel and Pregel. Gelnhausen told his wretched bawdy tales and decanted clownish wisdom in three different dialects, for in the course of the war Stoffel had acquired the Westphalian and Alemannic stammer on top of his native Hessian.

Though they spoke a confusing variety of languages, they made themselves clearly understood, and their German was free and unfettered. But that did not detract from their prowess in linguistic theory. No line of poetry but was subjected to some rule.

5

When Simon Dach gave the signal, the company moved with astonishing discipline from the taproom to the great hall; to him the poets subordinated their often childish willfulness. They accepted his authority. Rist and Zesen forsook (for a while) their deep-rooted contentiousness. Greflinger had always longed for such a father. It genuinely amused the aristocrat Hofmannswaldau to sacrifice his habits to the commoner Dach. The princes of learning—Harsdörffer with residence in Nuremberg, Buchner of Wittenberg—would gladly (under the warming influence of wine) have chosen Dach as their regent. And because for some years Weckherlin, who had grown bilious at court, had no longer been serving the King of England but had become a secretary of state under Parliament, he inclined to the will of the majority; along with the rest he acceded to Dach's sign, meanwhile uttering an ironic comment on the democratic puritanism of his elective home, where a certain Cromwell had turned poets into fire-eaters.

Only the student Scheffler had absented himself. While the company were still on their soup, he had wandered off through the Ems Gate and into town. There he went looking for the goal of the annual pilgrimage to Telgte, a wood-carved Pietà: Mary sitting stiffly, holding the death-stiffened body of her son.

When all had gathered in a semicircle around Dach, on benches and chairs and, these being insufficient, on milking stools and beer kegs under the beamed ceiling, the summer came in to them for a while through the open windows, mingling its buzzing of flies with their expectant silence or whispered exchanges. Schneuber was trying to convince Zesen of something. Weckherlin was explaining to Greflinger how secret agents went about coding their reports, a skill he had acquired in the service of various masters. The landlady's two donkeys could be heard outside, and from farther away the tavern dogs.

Next to Dach, who had allowed himself an armchair, a stool stood in wait for the speaker of the moment. Symbolic emblems, such as were customary at regional gatherings—the palm of the Fruit-bearing Society, for instance—had not been set up and did not adorn the background. Perhaps in the interest of simplicity. Or possibly because no significant emblem had occurred to them. Maybe one would turn up later on.

Without making an introductory speech, but merely calling the assembly to order by clearing his throat, Dach called on the first speaker, Augustus Buchner, the elderly and in every muscle austere Saxon magister of letters, a man so incapable of expressing himself without lecturing that even his silence suggested a lecture. He could be so ponderously silent that his mute periods might have been cited as figures of speech.

From his *Short Guide to German Poetry,* a work widely distributed in manuscript copies, Buchner read the tenth chapter, entitled "On the Measure of Verses and Their Varieties." His remarks, which he regarded as supplementary to Opitz's theoretical writings, dealt with the proper use of "dactylic words," reproved old Ambrosius Lobwasser of blessed memory for "mixing incorrect *pedes* into his alexandrines," and gave examples of a form of dactylic ode, the last four lines of which were trochaic in the bucolic manner.

Buchner's contribution was sprinkled with bows to Opitz—who, however, had to be contradicted here and there—and with gibes at the absent Schottel, that "preceptor of princes," for his servility and his addiction to secret societies. Though Abraham von Franckenberg was not named, the word "Rosicrucian" was mentioned. Occasionally the speaker switched to scholarly Latin. Even when talking extemporaneously, he could quote just about anything. (In the Fruit-bearing Society, to which he belonged, he was known as The Enjoyed One.)

When Dach threw the floor open to disputation, no one wished at first to question Buchner's authority, though most of the gentlemen were versed in theory, skilled in their craft, metrically surefooted, attuned to argumentative cross fire, eloquent beyond measure, and inclined to contradict even when words of approval were on the tips of their tongues. Merely because Rist, taking the tone of the preacher that he was, termed all criticism of Opitz "depraved and reprehensible," Zesen, who had studied under Buchner, replied that those were the words of a man, namely, the Elbe Swan master of Opitzism, whose entire work was a dull-witted parroting of Opitz.

After Harsdörffer's learned defense of the Nuremberg pastorals, which had, he believed, been attacked by Buchner, and Weckherlin's observation that in spite of Opitz's interdiction, he had made correct use of dactylic words long before Buchner, Gryphius distilled a drop of bitterness: such poetic schools, he declared, could at best promote soulless prolixity; to which Buchner agreed, adding that for that reason he, unlike certain other teachers of literature, would refrain from publishing his lectures.

Next Dach called on Sigmund Birken, whose hair hung down to his shoulders in curls that were constantly taking on new life. His round face disclosed childlike eyes and moist, pouting lips. One wondered why so much beauty should have need of theory.

After Birken had read the twelfth chapter from the manuscript of his *German Rhetoric and Poetic Art,* consisting of rules for actors, prescribing that an author should put appropriate speech into the mouths of his characters—"thus children should speak childishly, old people wisely, women chastely and gently, heroes bravely and heroically, peasants crudely"—Greflinger and Lauremberg jumped on him. Nothing but boredom, they declared, could come of that! Typical of the Pegnitz school! Wishywashy! And Moscherosch scoffed: In what century was this young fop living?

Harsdörffer tried rather halfheartedly to help his protégé. Such dramatic rules, he said, were demonstrable in the ancients. Gerhardt praised Birken's rule that horrors should not be shown directly but, at most, narrated. Gryphius, though said to be working on tragedies, was nevertheless silent. And Buchner's silence thundered menacingly.

At that point Gelnhausen asked for the floor. No longer swaggering in a green doublet with gold buttons, but (like Greflinger) wearing the baggy breeches of a soldier, he sat on one of the window seats and fidgeted impatiently until

Dach gave him leave to speak. He wished only, said Stoffel, to observe that to his higgledy-piggledy knowledge old people often talked childishly, children wisely, women crudely, and peasants chastely, whereas even on the point of death the heroes he had known spoke profanely. Only the Devil had spoken gently to him, usually at crossroads. Whereupon the regimental secretary gave an extemporaneous sampling of the speech of the persons cited, concluding with the Prince of Hell.

Even Gryphius laughed. And Dach closed the disputation on a conciliatory note by throwing out the question: was it advisable, since life confronted us daily with bloody deeds and obscenity, to show them on the stage as well? He himself, he held, was inclined to agree with young Birken's rule, provided it were not applied too rigidly.

Then he called on Hans Michael Moscherosch, whose satires from the first part of his *Visions of Philander of Sittewald,* though published and widely known, were nevertheless received with pleasure, especially the mocking ditty:

Most every tailor, sad to say,
Dabbles in languages today,
Latin and French—why not Bulgarian?—
When in his cups, the dumb vulgarian . . .

This fell in with the general outrage at the mutilation of the German language, in whose impressionable soil the French, Spanish, and

41

Swedish campaigns had left their hoof and wheel marks.

When landlady Libuschka called in from the doorway to ask whether the *signores* would care for a *boccolino* of *rouge,* the company answered in all the foreign languages then current in Germany. Each of those present, even Gerhardt, proved a master of mumbo-jumbo parody. And Moscherosch, on the one hand a sturdy fellow apt to be the first to laugh at his own jokes, but on the other hand a man inclined to profundity and belonging to the Order of the Palm Tree, in which he bore the epithet of The Dreamer, gave further samples of his satirical prowess. He scoffed at forced rhymes and pastoral circumlocutions. Without naming names he struck blows at the Pegnitz school. Several times he called himself a "good German," even though his name was of Moorish origin, as he pointed out for the benefit of anyone who might be toying with the thought of a rhyme for "stew." (It so happened that the bottom-of-the-barrel wine that the landlady had her maids serve was of Spanish origin.)

Then, from the just-printed first part of his *Poetic Funnel,* Harsdörffer read instructions as to the best way of handling his crash course for future poets—"After all, the six hours need not be successive and on the same day"—and then won general applause by taking out a manuscript and reading a brief encomium on the German language, which "more than any foreign tongue could imitate the sound and note of every creature, for it . . . whirs like the swallow, croaks like the raven, chirps like the sparrow, lisps and whispers with the flowing brook. . . ."

Obviously, we could never have come to any agreement as to whether to write *"teutsch"* or *"deutsch,"* but any praise of the German language in either spelling gave us a lift. Each of us thought up some new nature-imitating onomatopoeia to demonstrate the German art of word making. Soon (to Buchner's irritation) we were discussing Schottel's catalogue of linguistic inventions and praising his "snowy-milk-white" and other finds. When it came to improving the language and Germanizing foreign words, we found ourselves in agreement. Even Zesen's suggestion of replacing "convent" with *"Jungfernzwinger"* ("virgins' dungeon") met with approval.

It took Lauremberg's long poem, "Of Old-fashioned Poetry and Rhymes," which struck vigorous Low German blows at the new-fashioned High German, to divide the company again, though Lauremberg was a hard man to argue with. He knew his adversaries' arguments in advance—"Our language is accepted By every chancellery; Wherever German speech is written, High German it must be"—and praised his unspoiled Nether German as against the stilted, affected, now euphuistic, now bombastic chancellery, or High, German: "So stiff and glumpish one can scarce determine, Whether it's French or honest German."

Yet not only the modernists Zesen and Birken, but Buchner and Logau as well, rejected all dialects as vehicles of poetry. High German alone, they held, should be developed into an instrument of ever-increasing refinement, which would succeed—where sword and pike had failed—in sweeping the fatherland clean of foreign domination. Rist submitted that in that case it would be necessary to do away with all such old-fashioned claptrap as sacrilegious invocations of the Muses and references to those abominable heathen gods. Gryphius declared that, in opposition to Opitz, he had long held that dialects were needed to give force to the "main" language, but that since his studies in Leiden he had, not without regret, become stricter in his usage.

It was again Gelnhausen who, from the window seat, informed the company that whether, on the banks of the Rhine, people said *"Kappes,"* or between the Ems and the Weser said *"Kumst,"* cabbage was meant in either case. The linguistic controversy, he said, made no sense to him, but Lauremberg's poem had demonstrated to the satisfaction of every ear that Low German speech could lend winning sound to stilted discourse. Therefore, in his opinion, they should subsist side by side and mixed, and people so intent on cleanliness that the broom was never out of reach would end up sweeping life away.

Rist and Zesen wanted (both in alliance and opposition to each other) to raise objections, but Dach supported Stoffel.

44

He, too, he submitted, let his native Prussian flow like buttermilk into some of his lighter songs, and he had collected songs sung by the common people, hoping, with the help of Albert the organist, to make them suitable for singing by the general public. He then began to sing some of his verses in an undertone—"Annie of Tharaw, my true love of old, She is my life and my goods and my gold"—and after a while he was not singing alone, but in chorus with Lauremberg, Greflinger, Rist, and even with Gryphius's mighty voice, until at last Annie of Samland put an end to the linguistic controversy: "The threads of our two lives are woven in one."

Thereupon Simon Dach suspended the congress for that day. Dinner, he announced, was served in the taproom; if anyone found it too modest, he should bear in mind that a Croatian foraging party had only recently requisitioned the landlady's provisions, driven off her calves, slaughtered her hogs, and consumed or, to put it bluntly, gobbled up her last goose. Nevertheless, there would be plenty to eat. . . . And hadn't the afternoon given them pleasure with its argument and counterargument?

When they left the great hall, the medical student was back among them. His eyes were as wide as if he had beheld a miracle, but all that had happened was that the priest of the church had shown him the Telgte Pietà, which was hidden in a barn. To Czepko, who was standing beside him, Scheffler said that the Mother of God had told him that just as God was in him, she was in every maiden's womb.

6

What the landlady bade her maids dish up was not so very meager: steaming millet porridge in deep wooden bowls, with rendered lard and bits of bacon poured over it. On the side, boiled sausages and coarse bread. In addition, her garden, which lay behind the house, protected by the wilderness that fenced it round (which the Croatian foragers must have overlooked), had yielded onions, carrots, and black radishes, all of which were served raw and tasted good with the brown beer.

The company praised the simple fare. Even those ordinarily spoiled and pampered declared fulsomely that their palates had not enjoyed such blessings in a long, long time. Weckherlin excoriated English cooking. Hofmannswaldau called the rustic offering a meal for the gods.

Alternately in Latin and German, Harsdörffer and Birken spoke of comparable meals recorded in classical pastorals. And in the word flux of the Wedel pastor, Rist, whom Dach had appointed to say grace, the Emsland millet porridge was transformed into manna from heaven.

Only Gelnhausen first muttered to himself, then loudly reproved the landlady: What did Courage think she was doing! He could never expect his horsemen and musketeers, meanly lodged in her stable, to eat such swill more than once! If they remained loyal to the emperor, it was in the expectation of daily roast chicken, breast of beef, and jowl of pork, for, as everyone knew, their pay was inadequate. If the food served them wasn't crispy-succulent enough, they'd be serving the Swedes tomorrow. For just as a musket demanded dry powder, so a musketeer had to be kept in a good humor. And if Mars withdrew his protection, the swan-throated Apollo would find himself at the mercy of every reckless snickersnee. Meaning that without a military guard the poets' disputation couldn't last a day. He felt in duty bound to inform the gentlemen, as forbearingly as possible, not only—as Courage was well aware—that all Westphalia, especially the Tecklenburg area, was rich in forests and thickets, but also that the river Ems was crawling with highwaymen from end to end.

He then withdrew with Libuschka, who apparently recognized that Gelnhausen's horsemen and musketeers required additional sustenance.

Left alone for a while, the literary men, some frightened and others indignant at Gelnhausen's impudence, relieved their feelings in disputation. Never fear. They would manage to forget the danger facing their meeting through skillful recourse to the dactylic words for which they were always searching; the world could come to an end, and in the midst of the rumbling and roaring these gentlemen would quarrel over the correct or incorrect use of metric feet. In the last analysis—and Gryphius, with the verbal splendor of his sonnets, was not alone in having said so—all was vanity.

And so the company were soon back at the table, chewing and spooning in literary converse. At one end—facing Dach—Buchner, gesticulating as he spoke, expressed his suspicion of the absent Schottel, whom he accused of a coup against the Fruit-bearing Society. Whereupon Harsdörffer and his publisher, Endter, who had made secret arrangements with Schottel, parodied the magister's manner of speaking. On all sides the absent were thoroughly vilipended, quarrels crisscrossed, mockery was overdone, conferees belabored one another with stones transmuted into words. One group, straddling their bench, kept captious count of Lauremberg's Low German *"pedes"*: in another corner Zesen and Birken reviled the late Opitz, whose rules were termed relentless fences and whose images were disparaged as colorless. Both modernists accused Rist, Czepko, and (in covert whispers) Simon Dach of perpetual "Opitzizing."

On the other hand, Rist, who was sitting with Weckherlin and Lauremberg, waxed indignant over the immorality of the Pegnitz Shepherds: why, in Nuremberg, they were even admitting women to the sessions of the Order of Flowers. A good thing Dach hadn't invited any ladies, considering how fashionable their rhymed soul-mush had become.

Still others were standing around the seated Gryphius, who, though only thirty, was already well upholstered on all sides, bloated no doubt by grief and disgust with the world. His coat stretched tight in many places. His double chin, already betokening a third. He spoke with the voice of a prophet and could thunder even when he lacked lightning. In a small circle, he invoked humanity, and as he spoke the question—What is man?—found answer in ever-renewed images, each of which expunged the last: delusion on all sides. Gryphius dealt annihilation. Everything he did disgusted him. For all his impetuous need to write, he was perpetually, in a torrent of words, abjuring literature. At the same time, his disgust with everything written, let alone printed, went hand in hand with his eagerness to see everything he had recently poured forth—certain tragedies, for example, and various projected comedies or satires—published without delay. That is why, hardly a moment after pondering grandiloquent scenes, he was able without transition to bid farewell to "letters and all such trumpery," for no sooner do they come into being than decay sets in. Now that peace was in the offing, he declared, he preferred to make himself useful. The Glogau Estates had long been urging him to become their syndic. Though he had formerly abominated Opitz's only too adroit diplomacy, today he deemed activity conducive to the commonweal all the more indispensable. At a time when law and morality, even more than the devastated countryside, were everywhere in ruins, the prime imperative was to put order into chaos, for order alone could provide a blindly errant people with something to hold on to. Flowery pastorals and euphonious verses would accomplish nothing.

Such talk of abjuring the written word provoked Logau, who was standing to one side, to emit maxims all ready for the printer. If the shoemaker were to turn baker, he observed, the upshot would be leathery bread. And Weckherlin said that his almost thirty years of toil in the government service meant less to him than a single one of his odes, which he intended, the new ones along with those that were feeble with age, to send to the printer's soon.

And undeterred by Gryphius, who continued in ever-new images to proclaim the death of literature and the order-fostering rule of reason, the publishers, who had hitherto maintained a certain reserve, now went weaseling around the room in quest of promising manuscripts. Weckherlin's new book had already been placed in Amsterdam. Moscherosch lent ear to the advances of Naumann, the Hamburg bookseller. After as good as closing a deal with Rist, whose works had hitherto appeared in Lüneburg, for a voluminous manuscript celebrating the forthcoming peace, the publisher Endter vied with Mülbe of Strassburg and Elzevihr of Holland in trying to persuade the resourceful Hofmannswaldau to procure for them—that is, for one of the three—the manuscript of the deceased Jesuit Spee's *The Nightingale's Rival*, for, they said, provided it had merit, they would be willing to publish the work of a Papist. Hofmannswaldau held out hope to all three and allegedly—so Schneuber vituperated later on—accepted advances from all three. Nevertheless, *The Nightingale's Rival* by Friedrich von Spee was not published until 1649, and then by Friessem in Catholic Cologne.

So the evening waxed. A few of the gentlemen were moved to take the air in the landlady's garden but were soon driven back by the veils of gnats blown in from the Ems. Dach was amazed at the stubborn industry of Libuschka, who, warring with nettles and thistles, had managed to grow vegetables in the wilderness. With just such courage his friend Albert had induced his little garden to grow around the cucumber bower. Nothing remained of it. Soon there would be nothing left to praise but the thistle, that latter-day flower and symbol of adverse times.

Then they stood for a while in the courtyard or stretched their legs in the direction of the outer Ems, where stood an abandoned fulling mill. From there they were able to see that their meeting was being held on an island (Emshagen by name) separated from the town, between the two arms of the river. They spoke knowingly of the damaged, towerless town wall and admired Moscherosch's tobacco pipe. They chatted with the maids, one of whom (like the late Fleming's beloved) was named Elsabe, and, while the tavern dogs cavorted around them, apostrophized the tethered mules in Latin. They made biting or comical remarks against or about one another and argued a while as to whether, according to Schottel's instructive color scale, Libuschka's hair should be termed "pitch" or "coal" black, or whether it was permissible to characterize the early dusk as "donkey-fallow." They laughed at Greflinger, who, standing with legs wide-planted like a Swedish ensign, was telling the musketeers about his campaigns under Baner and Torstenson. Several groups were about to stroll down the Hauptstrasse in the direction of the Ems Gate—for the town of Telgte was still unknown to them—when one of the imperial horsemen of Stoffel's guard rode into the courtyard and handed a message to Gelnhausen, who was standing in the stable doorway with the landlady and the sergeant of musketeers. It was soon known to all that Trauttmannsdorff, the emperor's chief negotiator, had suddenly—on the sixteenth day of July—left Münster in manifestly high spirits and set out for Vienna, to the discomfiture of the conference and all its participants.

In a trice the conversation turned political and moved to the taproom, where a fresh keg of brown beer was opened. Only the youngsters—Birken, Greflinger, and, hesitantly, the student Scheffler—stayed in the courtyard with Zesen and approached the maids. Each made a grab or (in Scheffler's case) was grabbed; Zesen alone was left empty-handed, and, his feelings hurt by Greflinger's mockery, went down to the river. He wanted to be alone with himself.

But no sooner had I caught sight of him standing above the outer Ems, which had dug deep into its sandy bed, than two corpses, tied together, were washed against the bank. Though bloated, they could be recognized as a man and a woman. After brief hesitation—an eternity for Zesen—the pair broke loose from the tangled reeds, spun around playfully in the current, escaped from the eddy, and glided downstream to the mill weir where evening was blending into night, leaving nothing behind except potential metaphors, which Zesen began at once to pad with resounding neologisms. He was so hard pressed by language that he had no time to be horrified.

7

In the taproom conjectures were exchanged over beer. His smile—since Trauttmannsdorff passed for a gloomy man—could only be interpreted as a sign of Papist triumph, Habsburg advantage, new loss for the Protestant camp, and further postponement of the peace—such were the opinions with which the gentlemen added to one another's fears. Especially the Silesians saw themselves forsaken. Czepko had a foreboding that they would all be abandoned to the Jesuits.

They edged away from Gelnhausen, who made light of the imperial legate's sudden departure. What, he asked, was there to be surprised at, when you stopped to think that ever since Wrangel had replaced the gout-ridden Torstenson, he had done nothing but carry on private warfare to fill his pockets, preferring an invasion of Bavaria in quest of spoils to a march on Vienna through gaunt Bohemia. Nor were the French doing very well by the Protestant cause, now that—according to a street song current in Paris—Anne of Austria was darning Mazarin's socks while the cardinal was anointing her royal courage.*

Exactly, cried Libuschka; she had known the score ever since she had lost her maidenhead. Seven times she had been married, mostly to imperial, but also to Hessian cavalry captains, and once almost to a Dane. And each time, whether a priest or a Lutheran minister had blessed the union, she had been used and reviled as a "courage." That's the military for you, as bad on one side as on the other. And Stoffel here—whom everybody, first in Hanau, later in Soest, and then again at the spa where they had gone to cure the love pox—had addressed as Simpel—Run, Simpel! Come here, Simpel! Hurry up, Simpel!—had no more in his codpiece than her dear departed captains.

*How did "courage" get to mean the female sex organ and by extension a peddler of the same? And how, for that matter, did Libuschka come to be known as Courage? Thereby hangs a tale. As a young girl Libuschka, to protect her virginity from the imperial troops who had occupied the Bohemian town of Bragoditz, where she lived, dressed as a boy, took the name of Janko, and went to work as a groom for a German cavalryman, who soon passed her on to a captain. Libuschka-Janko served the captain well, acquired the ways of a fighting man, and even took part in foraging expeditions. One day she got into a fight with another groom, who had insulted the Bohemian nation. When her antag-

"You shut your trap, Courage, or I'll shut it for you!" Gelnhausen shouted. Didn't she know that an account had been open since their course of medical treatment in Swabia?

She'd open an account for him, all right, she replied; she'd make him pay for all the brats born in his wake in one garrison town after another.

What, he cried, was this nonsense about brats? When she, Courage, had never brought any brats into the world, but sat barren on a donkey that ate nothing but thistles. She herself was a thistle that needed to be hacked out wherever it grew. Roots and all!

Whereupon landlady Libuschka, as though Gelnhausen had actually taken a knife to her, jumped on the table among the beer mugs, stamped till the beer mugs danced, suddenly picked up her skirts, dropped her breeches, turned her arse in Stoffel's direction, and gave him a well-aimed answer.

"Hey, Gryf!" cried Moscherosch. "What do

onist tried to grab her "by the utensil which she had not," her fear of being unmasked redoubled her strength and she gave him a sound thrashing. The story came to the captain's ears. To continue in Libuschka's own words: "When he asked me why I had beaten the fellow so villainously, I replied: 'Because he grabbed at my courage, where no man's hand had ever ventured before.' You see, I wanted to express myself allusively and not with Swabian crudeness. . . . And since my virginity was on its last legs in any case, for that groom would surely have betrayed me, I bared my snow-white bosom and showed the captain my hard, alluring breasts." Grimmelshausen, *Lebensbeschreibung der Erzbetrügerin und Landstörzerin Courasche.*—TRANS.

you think of that? What splendid dialogues and curtain scenes the writers of German tragedies could cull from her!"

Everyone laughed. Even from Gryphius, who a moment before had been deep in gloom, laughter erupted. Weckherlin wanted to hear "Courage's thunder" again. And after Logau had delivered himself of a maxim to the effect that a fart had deeper meaning than the sound might suggest, the company soon recovered from the dismay caused by Trauttmannsdorff's sudden departure. (Only Paul Gerhardt sought out his room in horror. For he had an intimation of the turn that the landlady's nether wind would give the gentlemen's conversation.)

Over their brown beer they treated one another to crude and double-meaningful anecdotes. Moscherosch had several unprinted calendars full of them in readiness. With turns of phrase that obscured more than they revealed, Hofmannswaldau related how shamelessly Opitz had carried on with several daughters of Breslau burghers, yet avoided paying alimony. Old Weckherlin drained the sink of London's iniquity, taking special pleasure in exhibiting the nakedness of the Puritan hypocrites, the new ruling class. From Schneuber the company learned the intimate secrets of aristocratic ladies who, in frequenting the Society of the Pine Tree, had not only couched their thoughts in rhyme but had also couched themselves with Rompler and his friends. Naturally Lauremberg contributed. Everyone opened his tap. Even

Gryphius, inclining to pressure, served up a few tidbits brought back from his trip to Italy, for the most part anecdotes about whoring monks, which Harsdörffer tried to outdo and Hofmannswaldau embroidered into stories about triangles and squares: this exercise gave them occasion to display their learning, for, in introducing or winding up a tale about bumptious trollops or randy monks, they would indicate their French or Italian sources.

When the amazed Simon Dach remarked that he evidently lived in the wrong place, since he could report no such happenings from Königsberg-Kneiphof, where the goings-on were sometimes crude but never so outrageous, his contribution was found particularly amusing. And if, prodded by Harsdörffer and others, landlady Libuschka and Gelnhausen (temporarily reconciled) had not told a few stories, he from his life as a soldier—the Battle of Wittstock—she from her days as a sutler at the camp outside Mantua, and then a few bawdy tales from their time together at the spa, the evening would have gone on merrily with storytelling and keg tapping. But when the two of them lined up the gruesome particulars of what had happened in Magdeburg when Tilly and his butchers fell on the city, the listeners were numbed; brazenly Libuschka told them how much she had gained in the looting. She boasted of baskets full of gold chains she had cut off the necks of slaughtered women. In the end Gelnhausen poked her to make her stop. Magdeburg's suffering admitted of no reaction but silence.

Speaking into the stillness, Dach said it was late, time for sleep. Stoffel's and especially Libuschka's unvarnished report, which had thoughtlessly been asked of them, showed, said Dach, where laughter had to stop and how dearly we pay for too much laughter, with the result that they all, with their laughter in their throats, were driven to gulping. And this had happened because horror had become a commonplace even to persons of sensibility. May the Lord forgive them and favor them in His mercy.

Dach sent the company to bed like children, without even the nightcap that Lauremberg and Moscherosch tried to insist on. He wanted to hear no more laughter, however subdued. Enough wit had been squandered. Luckily, he said, the pious Gerhardt had gone early to his room. Rist—ordinarily a vigorous preacher—ought really to have put a stop to the verbal whoring. No, he wasn't angry with anyone, he, too, had joined in the laughter. For the present there was nothing more to be said. But tomorrow, when manuscripts would again be read for the benefit of all, he hoped, as anyone who knew him would testify, to be of good cheer with the rest of them.

When all was still in the house—except for the landlady, who was putting her kitchen in order and most likely had Gelnhausen with her—Simon Dach passed once again through the corridors and looked in at the attic, where the youngsters were bedded on straw. There they lay, and the maids were with them. Birken lay held in arms like a child. How deeply they had exhausted themselves. Only Greflinger started up and wanted to explain. But Dach motioned him with his fingers to stay quiet and under his blanket. Let them enjoy themselves. If anyone had sinned, it was not here in the straw, but in the taproom. (And I had joined in the laughter, I had let stories occur to me, I had started the trouble, and—once it was started—I had willingly sat in the seat of the scornful.) After casting a last look, Dach was glad to see that the bashful Scheffler had ended up with one of the maids.

When at last he started back to his room— possibly to write a letter—he heard horses, wagon wheels, the dogs, and then voices in the courtyard. That must be my Albert, Dach hoped.

8

He did not come alone. The Königsberg cathedral organist, who had made a name for himself well beyond the borders of Prussia as a composer and a publisher and was known in particular for the successive volumes of his "arias," was accompanied by his cousin Heinrich Schütz, *Kapellmeister* at the court of Saxony, who was on his way to Hamburg and then to Glückstadt, where he hoped to find a long-coveted invitation to the Danish court. There was nothing more to keep him in Saxony. In his early sixties like Weckherlin, but more robust than the Swabian, who had worn himself out in government service, Schütz was a man of austere authority and stern grandeur, whom no one (except Albert, and he only in part) could fathom. His presence—far from overbearing, he seemed troubled by fear of being in the way—raised the tone of the poets' gathering but at the same time reduced the measure of its importance. A man whom no group could endure had come to their meeting.

I won't claim to be wiser than I was then—but everyone knew that, little as Schütz questioned his God and devoted as he had proved to his prince in spite of repeated Danish offers, his only true allegiance was to his own aspirations. Never, even in his incidental compositions, had he achieved the mediocrity required by Protestants for their daily use. He had provided neither his elector nor Christian of Denmark with anything more than the strictest minimum of courtly music. Though still as active as in the prime of life, he rejected the usual busyness. When the publishers of his works insisted on additions conducive to use in the churches, such as the notation of the thorough bass, Schütz, in his prefaces, deplored these adjuncts and warned against their use, since in his opinion the basso continuo should never be anything but a rarely used expedient.

Since he attached more importance than did any other composer to the written word, and since his music was designed to serve and interpret the word, to enhance it, underline its gestures, and give it greater depth, breadth, and elevation, Schütz was strict with words and confined himself for the most part either to the traditional Latin liturgy or to the text of Luther's

Bible. In his main work, his religious music, he had thus far eschewed the productions of contemporary poets, with the exception of Becker's *Psalter* and a few of the poems written by Opitz in his youth; urgently as he had appealed to us for texts, the German poets had nothing to offer him. Consequently, when Simon Dach heard his guest's name, his first feeling, before he could experience pleasure, was one of alarm.

They stood for a while in the courtyard, exchanging *politesses*. Over and over again Schütz apologized for arriving uninvited. As though to justify himself, he observed that he had been acquainted for years with some of the gentlemen (Buchner, Rist, Lauremberg). Dach, for his part, tried to put into words the honor that was being shown them. Gelnhausen's imperial guard stood in the background, holding torches. The musketeers thought they were witnessing the arrival of a prince, though Schütz's travel costume was that of a burgher and his luggage could be carried in two hands. (The other guest, they believed, must be the prince's gentleman-in-waiting.)

The travelers had come by way of Oesede, where they had found the instructions to proceed to Telgte. Since Schütz was traveling with a safe-conduct signed by the Elector of Saxony, there had been no difficulty in securing fresh horses. As though to identify himself, he showed the document with an almost childlike pride, meanwhile talking of one thing and another: an uneventful trip, with nothing untoward to report;

the flat countryside had been well lighted by the full moon; the fields were fallow, overgrown with weeds; he was more tired than hungry; he would gladly sleep on the stove bench if no bed was available; he knew all about inns, for his father had been the landlord of the Schützenhof in Weissenfels on the Saale, which was often full beyond capacity.

With difficulty Dach and Albert persuaded the *Kapellmeister* to move into Dach's room. When the landlady appeared (with Gelnhausen in the background) and heard the guest's name, she hastened to greet him in a burst of Italian as Maestro Sagittario.* All were even more surprised (and Schütz a little shaken) when Gelnhausen, after serviceably stationing himself beside the newcomer's luggage, began in a pleasing tenor to sing the first motet of the *Cantiones sacrae,* a supradenominational work which had accordingly circulated in Catholic as well as Protestant regions: *"O bone, o dulcis, o benigne Jesu . . ."*

And Stoffel explained that while serving as a baggage boy in Breisach when the town was being besieged by the Weimar troops, he had sung in the choir, because singing made hunger more bearable. Then he picked up the luggage and drew Schütz and all the others after him. The landlady came last, taking a jug of apple cider and some black bread to the newcomer's room at his request.

Sagittario is Italian and *Schütze* is German for "archer."—TRANS.

Later Libuschka made up a makeshift bed in the taproom for Dach and Albert, who had declined to take over her alcove beside the kitchen. She addressed her flow of talk chiefly to Albert: how hard it was in such times for an unattached woman to preserve her honor; how beautiful she had been in former days, and what sufferings had made her wiser. . . . In the end Stoffel dragged her out of the room. A very special cement knitted him and Courage together.

No sooner had the two of them gone than the guests were again disturbed. Zesen's horrified face appeared in the open window on one side of the taproom. He had come from the river, he spluttered; it was full of corpses; first he had seen just two of them; they had been tied together, and that reminded him of his Markhold and Rosemunde; then more and more had come drifting down; the moon had lighted their floating flesh; he could find no words for so much death; the house was beset by evil omens; there would never be peace; because the language had not been kept pure; because mutilated words had swelled up like drifting corpses. He would write what he had seen. Just that. Immediately. He would find tones that had never before been heard.

Dach closed the window. Finally, after listening to Zesen first with horror, then with amusement, the two friends were alone. Time and again they embraced each other, now and then slapping each other's back and grumbling rough-hewn terms of endearment that could never have been fitted into dactylic meter. Though only a short while ago Dach, to punish the company for their smutty stories, had sent them to their rooms without a nightcap, he now filled mugs with brown beer for himself and Albert. Several times they touched mug to mug.

When the two friends lay in the dark, the organist told Dach what a hard time he had had persuading Schütz to come. His distrust of writers and their far too many words had increased in the last few years. When Rist had provided him with nothing and Lauremberg's libretti had served him poorly at the Danish court, he had taken up one of Schottel's operas, but Schottel's stilted verbiage still disgusted him. So it was not love for his kinsman that had moved Albert's world-famous cousin to detour via Telgte, but the hope that Gryphius might read some dramatic work that would supply him with the text for an opera. And Albert reiterated the hope that one manuscript or another might find grace in the eyes of his exacting cousin.

Simon Dach worried as he lay in the darkness; would his motley and quarrelsome literary circus—the wild Greflinger, the testy Gerhardt, so ready, as he had just shown, to take umbrage, the disturbed Zesen—would they behave with adequate decorum in the presence of so distinguished a visitor?

In the midst of his worries sleep overcame him. Only the beams of the Bridge Tavern remained awake. Or did something else happen during the night?

9

In the room that he shared with his counterpart, Rist, Zesen continued for quite some time to line up sonorous words until he fell asleep over a line in which swollen, ballooning corpses were likened to Rosemunde's flesh and his own.

In the meantime a courier from Osnabrück rode across the Ems and past the Bridge Tavern on his way to Münster, and another rode in the opposite direction; both were carrying news that would be stale by the time it reached its destination. The tavern dogs barked.

Then, after looking down on the river for a long time, the full moon stood over the tavern and its guests. No one evaded its influence. From it emanated change.

That must be why the three couples in the attic straw bedded themselves in different and contrary wise; for when they awoke in the gray of dawn, Greflinger, who at the start of his night in the straw had lain with the dainty and delicate maid, now found himself with the bony one, whose name was Marthe. And the plump maid, Elsabe by name, who had lain at first with the retiring Scheffler, found herself lying with Birken, whereas the dainty and delicate maid, Marie, who had fallen at first to Greflinger's lot, now lay asleep as though bound by chains to Scheffler. When they woke one another up and (moved by the moon) saw themselves wrongly paired, they didn't wish to lie as they were, but they no longer knew exactly with whom they had originally tumbled into the straw. After another change, it is true, each man and his maid thought they were lying right, but the full moon, which had long changed its place, was still exerting its influence. As though called by the unfaithful Flora, who had given his songs their sheen but had for years been the wedded wife of another, Greflinger, who had black hair covering the whole length of his back, crawled to the plump Elsabe; the dainty and delicate Marie flung herself on the pouting, angelic lips of Birken, who always, whether with the bony, the plump, or the dainty and delicate maid, thought he was lying with a nymph; and the tall, rawboned Marthe forced Scheffler between her limbs, in order, as previously the plump maid and the dainty and delicate maid had done, to fulfill the promise that the wooden Telgte Madonna had given

70

him the day before. And time and time again the frail young student poured out his soul with his sperm.

So it came about that for the third time all six began to thresh the attic straw, after which each was acquainted with each; no wonder that the bedfellows failed to hear what else happened that early morning.

But I know. Five horsemen led their saddled mounts out of the stable and into the courtyard. Gelnhausen was there. No door squeaked, no iron struck stone. The horses trod slowly and silently. Their hoofs had been wrapped in rags. And with sure hands—no leather slapped, the shafts were well oiled on their pins—two musketeers harnessed one of the covered wagons that the imperial troops had requisitioned in Oesede. A third brought muskets for himself and the other two and thrust them under the canvas. No need for words. Everything went off as though rehearsed. Not a murmur out of the tavern dogs.

Only the landlady of the Bridge Tavern whispered something to Gelnhausen, instructions no doubt, for Stoffel, already mounted, punctuated her words with nods of the head. As though playing a part, Libuschka (formerly known as Courage) stood wrapped in a horse blanket beside the sometime huntsman of Soest, who still (or once again) looked dashing in a green doublet with gold buttons and a plumed hat.

Only Paul Gerhardt woke up when the team tugged at the covered wagon and the emperor's horsemen rode out of the courtyard. He was just in time to see Gelnhausen turn in his saddle, draw his sword, and with his free hand wave laughingly at the landlady, who made no sign in answer, but was still standing stiffly in the courtyard, wrapped in her blanket, when the wagon and riders were curtained off by the alders before being swallowed up by the Ems Gate.

Then the birds started in. Or perhaps it was only then that Gerhardt heard how many birds had been ushering in the Telgte morning. Larks, finches, blackbirds, titmice, starlings. In the elderberry bushes behind the stable, in the copper beech in the middle of the courtyard, in the four lime trees that had been planted on the weather side of the tavern, from the birch and alder woods invaded by the scrub from the outer bank of the Ems, also in the nests the sparrows had built themselves in the weather-beaten thatched roof that was falling apart around the rear gable. From all directions the morning began with birds. (There were no cocks left in the town.)

When landlady Libuschka broke loose from her freeze and slowly, shaking her head and muttering plaintively, shuffled out of the courtyard, she, who the day before had raucously set the tone and had still impressed the gentlemen as a valid target, became an old woman; abandoned to herself, wrapped in her horse blanket.

For which reason Paul Gerhardt, who now started on his morning prayers, included poor

Courage in his plea: he prayed that the Lord and merciful Father might not in His wrath punish the wretched woman too severely for her sins; that He might look with forbearance upon her future trespasses, for the war had made this poor woman what she was and corrupted many another pious soul besides her. Then he prayed, as he had every morning for years, that peace might come soon, bringing safety to all true believers, and to the heretics, who denied the true God, either ultimate insight or merited punishment. Among the heretics the pious man numbered not only, as any orthodox Lutheran traditionally would have, the Catholics of the clerical party, but also the Huguenots, Zwinglians, Calvinists, and all mystical fantasts; for which reason the piety of the Silesian repelled him.

Gerhardt was truly pious only in his conception of God—and in his hymns, which carried farther than he in his bigotry would have liked. For years, ever since he had been tutoring children in Berlin and hoping vainly for a parsonage, simple words had come to him, few in number yet sufficient to provide Lutheran congregations with ever-new songs in rhymed stanzas, so that everywhere, in homes and in what churches the war had left standing (even in Catholic regions), people sang with the pious Gerhardt—in the old-fashioned manner and to the unassuming melodies of Crüger and later of Ebeling; his "Morning Song," for example— "Awake, my heart, and sing"—the last stanzas of which, "To the Creator of all things, the giver of all gifts, the guardian and protector ... ," had been written on the way to Telgte; all nine stanzas would shortly be set to music by Johann Crüger.

Even if Gerhardt had been able to, nothing and no one could have induced him to write anything else—odes, elegant sonnets, or satires, let alone lewd pastorals. He was not a literary man, and the folk song had given him more than he had learned from Opitz (and his executor Buchner). His hymns had nature in them and did not speak figuratively. Consequently, he had at first declined to attend the poets' meeting. It was solely as a favor to Dach, whose practical piety just barely fitted into Gerhardt's concept of religion, that he had agreed to come. But exactly as he had foreseen, he had immediately taken umbrage at everything and everyone: at Hofmannswaldau with his perpetual witty talk; at Gryphius with his self-satisfied, all-encompassing disgust of the world which he had not yet milked dry; at the muddled aestheticist prattle of the supposedly gifted Zesen; at the way Lauremberg kept serving up the same old satire; at Czepko's pansophic ambiguities; at Logau's blasphemous tongue; at Rist's bluster, and the busy comings and goings of the publishers. All that, the glib talk and perpetual know-it-allness of the literati, so repelled him that he stood by no one but himself (his obstinately independent mind), belonged to no literary group, and no sooner arrived than longed to go home; but the pious man stayed on.

And when Paul Gerhardt, after pleading for the salvation of the shameless landlady and the damnation of all enemies of the true faith, continued his morning prayer, he entreated the Lord at length to enlighten his Calvinist prince, who was summoning Huguenots and other heretics to the March of Brandenburg as settlers, for which reason Gerhardt could not love him. Then he included the poets in his prayer.

He begged the Almighty God and Father to endow the most learned but abysmally erring gentlemen—the worldly-wise Weckherlin and the shady (because of his dubious origins) Moscherosch, the wicked Greflinger and even the clownish Stoffel, though a Catholic—with right words. His fingers interlocked, he prayed with fervor that the congress might in all things praise the glory of God, the supreme judge.

As a postscript to his morning prayer, he begged that he might at long last be granted a parsonage, if possible in Brandenburg; but it was not until four years later that Paul Gerhardt became rural dean of Mittenwalde, where he was at last enabled to marry the already aging love of his tutorial days, his pupil Anna Berthold, and wrote hymn after hymn, all with many stanzas.

Then Simon Dach rang the bell in the taproom. All those who were still asleep woke up. The young men found themselves maidless in the attic straw. Marthe, Elsabe, and Marie were

75

already at work in the kitchen. They cut stale bread into the morning soup, of which Heinrich Schütz also partook after seating himself, a stranger though known to all, at the long table, between Gerhardt and Albert.

10

How radiantly that summer's day began. Light poured through every window, lending a touch of warmth to a house kept cool by the dampness of the walls. And the hour was also brightened by the joy of the conferees at the presence of their distinguished guest.

Immediately after the morning soup, still in the taproom (this time Czepko had said grace), Simon Dach stood up and addressed the company. Before they went back to their manuscripts, he said, it was fitting that a cordial welcome be given to the illustrious guest, but this, he felt, must be done by someone more proficient than himself, a mere music lover. His Albert—as he called the cathedral organist—was more at home with motets and madrigals, whereas he, Dach, for want of knowledge, could offer no more than wondering admiration. At the most he was able to appreciate ditties with thorough-bass accompaniments. Then he sat down, relieved.

After an elaborate exordium, Heinrich Albert sketched in the honored guest's career: How under the patronage first of the Landgrave of Kassel, then of the Elector of Saxony, young Schütz, though destined by his parents for the study of the law, had studied composition in Venice under the world-famous Gabrieli, whom he could have succeeded as organist in charge of both organs at St. Mark's basilica, but it had meant more to him to return to his own country. Not until much later, when war had begun to exact its murderous toll from Germany, had he gone back to Italy to continue his studies under the illustrious Monteverdi, after which, fully the great man's equal, he had returned with the most modern music, having so mastered his craft that he was now able to give voice to the joys and sorrows of men, their anguished silence and their anger, their weary waking and tormented sleep, their yearning for death and their fear of God, and not last to the praise of His goodness. All this, for the most part, according to the uniquely true words of Scripture. And in innumerable works: in religious concerti, in musical exequies, in his *Story of the Resurrection,* or—as recently as two years ago—in his setting of *The Seven Words on the Cross.* All these had been at once severe and tender, simple and artful. For which reason most of his works had proved too difficult for the common cantor or the scantily trained choral singer. He himself, Albert owned, had often despaired of Schütz's intricate polyphony, and had done so again only recently when, in preparation for the festival of the Reformation, he had attempted the Ninety-eighth Psalm—"Sing unto the Lord"—with his Kneiphof choir and had acknowledged failure in the face of its antiphony. However, he did not wish on so joyful an occasion to offend the master with the everlasting lament of the church organist, especially as the *Kapellmeister* knew from hard experience how difficult it was in times so long unsettled by war to keep competent singers and violinists. Even proud Dresden was wanting in instrumentalists. Receiving no proper pay, the foreign virtuosi sought the security and regularity that came from princely favor. He was barely able to feed his few boy choristers. Ah, if only God in His mercy would grant peace at long last, for then performers might once more be as skillful as the exacting master demanded.

Then, quite casually, Albert stated Schütz's request for leave to listen in at the manuscript reading, in the hope of being inspired at last to compose madrigals, as Monteverdi had done, to words in his own language, or of hearing some dramatic work on which to base an opera, just as twenty years past the late Opitz's *Dafne* had been amenable to his music; in which connection he felt that he still owed the here-present Magister Buchner a debt of thanks for his help as an intermediary.

All waited somewhat uneasily for the guest's answer, for all the time that Albert had been eulogizing the master, deploring his difficult mode of composition, and finally stating his wishes, nothing had happened in Schütz's face. The creases in his high, careworn forehead had not so much as deepened, let alone relaxed. His eyes were still focused every bit as attentively upon something sad, situated well outside the room. His mouth—under his mustache and above his beard, both of which were carefully cut in the manner of the long-dead Gustavus Adolphus—drooped at the corners. His grayish-brown hair, which he wore combed back. His immobility, scarcely stirred by his breathing.

When at last he spoke, his statement of thanks was brief. He had merely, he said, carried further what Johann Gabriel had taught him. The touch of childishness with which this always dignified man showed everyone at the table the ring that he wore on his left hand seemed strange, perhaps even a trifle absurd. Giovanni Gabrieli, he informed the company, had given him that ring just before his death. In a single sentence he disposed of the difficult polyphony Albert had mentioned: music, he said, required that sort of artistry, if it was to keep faith with the pure word of God. Then came a first judgment, spoken softly but audible the whole length of the table. Those who wished to make things easier for themselves and remain outside the domain of art could, he recommended, confine themselves to strophic songs with thorough-bass accompaniment. But now, he concluded, he was eager to hear something of which he himself was incapable—skillfully written words.

Schütz, who had spoken seated, stood up, so giving the signal, without Dach's having to speak again, for a general move into the spacious hall. All left the table; only Gerhardt hesitated, because he took Schütz's disparaging remarks about strophic songs as aimed solely at himself. Weckherlin had to plead with him and finally drag him into the other room.

Dach had other difficulties with Gryphius, who did not wish to read, and certainly not immediately, from the tragedy he had recently completed in Strassburg, on his way back from France. Very well, he would comply if need be, but not at that particular moment and not merely because Schütz—with all due respect to his greatness—so desired. Besides, he was no writer of operas, he lacked the passion for courtly pomp. Let Dach call on others first, perhaps on the youngsters. Apparently the night had not agreed with them. They were yawning in three parts and sagging at the knees. Even Greflinger was as silent as the tomb. Perhaps some of their own verse, sleepy as it might make others, would wake its authors.

All this made sense to Dach. But when Rist and Moscherosch asked leave to open the session with a manifesto that the two of them, assisted by Hofmannswaldau and Harsdörffer, had sat up drafting until late into the night and reworked in the morning—an appeal for peace to be addressed by the poets of Germany to their princes—the Königsberg magister feared for the cohesion of his literary family. "Later, friends!" he cried. "Later! First let us feed Master Schütz with our ink-stained labors. Politics is the gout-racked spouse of peace. She won't run away from us."

By then we were sitting in our usual places in the great hall. From outside we could hear, farther away than the day before, the mules tethered in the Emshagen wilderness. Someone (Logau?) asked where Stoffel was. Gerhardt kept silent. Not until Harsdörffer repeated the question did the landlady provide information: The regimental secretary had been called to Münster on pressing business. At the crack of dawn.

Libuschka had recovered her spirits. Light of foot, she was everywhere at once, now with curled hair. She had not spared the face paint. Her maids carried a comfortable easy chair with wide armrests into the semicircle. In the light from the window to one side of him, Heinrich Schütz sat as though upraised, presenting his careworn brow to the assembly.

11

It was still early morning when the second day of reading began. An ornament had now been placed beside the still-empty reader's stool: a tall thistle, dug from the landlady's garden and planted in an earthenware pot. Thus isolated and taken as a thing apart, the thistle was beautiful.

Without allusion to this "symbol of war-ravaged times," Dach proceeded to the order of the day. He had no sooner settled, with an air of old, established routine, in his chair facing the semicircle, than he called on the youngsters—Birken Scheffler Greflinger—to read successively from the stool at his side (now placed next to the thistle).

Sigmund Birken, a wartime child of Bohemian extraction, had fled to Nuremberg; welcomed by Harsdörffer, Klaj, and their group of Pegnitz Shepherds, he had met with idyllic support and encouragement in patrician homes and, as borne out by his reading of the previous day, had early given evidence of theoretical zeal. Under the name of Floridan in the Pegnitz Shepherds and known to Zesen's German-minded Association as The Sweet-smelling One, he had been applauded for his hymns, his prose and verse idylls, and his allegorical plays. Because of the enthusiastic reception given some years later to his Nuremberg production of a pageant entitled *The Departure of War and the Entrance of Peace into Germany* before a military audience, he was shortly thereafter ennobled by the emperor and received into the Order of the Palm Tree under the name of The Well-grown. Everywhere, at home and on his travels, he kept a succinct diary, for which reason his belongings, when he lodged in the attic straw of the Bridge Tavern, included a "Journal" ornamented with a flower-tendril design.

Birken the sound painter, for whom everything became sound and form and who, in keeping with the most modern sensibility, gave nothing its name but transposed everything into images, read a few painstakingly wrought, here bulging, there narrowing, figure poems in cross and heart shape, which were beautiful in appearance but called forth no applause from the company, because the form did not come out in the reading. More enthusiasm was aroused by a poem that, in playful words, made Peace and

Justice exchange kisses: ". . . the sweetest kisses are sweeter than sweet . . ."

What Harsdörffer and Zesen (the one learnedly, the other with high-flown interpretations) praised as epoch-making innovation gave Buchner occasion for long-winded misgivings, permitted Moscherosch to parody the poet's whole manner but most particularly the rhyme "sweating-fretting" in the heart-shaped poem, and almost made Rist jump out of his clerical skin. A good thing, he cried, that poor Opitz had been spared this "Zesenized Birkenry."

The "gracefully tumbling" words had appealed to old Weckherlin. Logau, as usual, expressed himself tersely. Where meaning was absent, he said, why shouldn't singsong and dingdong exchange compliments?

Next Johann Scheffler, who was soon to become a physician and later on, as a priest (under the name of Angelus Silesius), was to promote the Jesuit Counter-Reformation, sat beside the thistle. At first hesitating and muddling his words, then more composed, fortified no doubt by Czepko's "Chin up, student!," he read an early version of his hymn "Thee will I love, my strength, my tower," which came later on to be sung by all denominations. Then he recited a few epigrams that ten years later were to make their way in their definitive form under the title *Der cherubinische Wandersmann (The Cherubinic Wanderer)* but for the present puzzled the assembly, because no one, with the possible exception of Czepko and Logau, could make anything of lines such as "I know God cannot live an instant without me," not to mention "When God lay hid in womb of maiden chaste, The circle then was by the point embraced."

Gerhardt jumped up as though stung by a wasp: Another Silesian will-o'-the-wisp! That accursed shoemaker* still speaking out of the mouths of his pupils. Hocus-pocus and mystical rubbish! And he warned the gathering against the false glitter of God-abusing paradox.

As a pastor of the Wedel congregation, Rist felt called upon to agree, in a voice as though from the pulpit, with everything Gerhardt had said. But he refrained from putting it more plainly, since he suspected Papist poison hidden in the rubbish.

To the surprise of all, the Lutheran Gryphius put in a word for Scheffler. Alien as it was to him, he declared, the charm of this miraculously self-contained order was balm to his soul.

The next to read was Georg Greflinger, the object of Dach's paternal favor and solicitude, a tall, broad-shouldered young fellow whom the war had driven as a child from a sheep pasture to Regensburg, later forcing him into the Swedish service and making him so restless that he was constantly traveling between Vienna and Paris, Frankfurt, Nuremberg, and the Baltic towns, everywhere entangling himself in one love affair after another. Only recently his long-

*The Silesian mystic Jakob Böhme (1575–1624).—TRANS.

est engagement had been cast aside by the daughter of a Danzig artisan, who had thus become the faithless Flora of his poems. Not until the following year was he to marry in Hamburg, settle down, and embark on a profitable business career, for concurrently with devoting four thousand alexandrines to the history of the Thirty Years' War, he opened a news agency and, beginning in the late fifties, published a weekly newspaper, the *Nordische Mercur*. Wholly concerned with earthly matters, Greflinger recited two bawdy ditties, the one wittily praising infidelity—"When Flora was jealous"— the other rollicking—"Hylas doesn't want a wife"—and both well suited to being read out loud. While the young man, parodying himself and his military bearing, was still declaiming his jests, the assembly was seized with merriment. The lines "No one girl is enough for me, Whoring, whoring, whoring is my life" were followed by modest laughter. The restraint was all for the benefit of Schütz. Though Dach and Albert were both amused, they did not contradict Gerhardt when, in the ensuing discussion period, he took exception to the praise meted out by Moscherosch and Weckherlin. Such doggerel, he said, was only fit for the gutter. Were they trying to bring down God's wrath on the heads of the assembly?

Heinrich Schütz sat silent.

Then came a disturbance, for the landlady's three maids, who (with Dach's permission) had been listening at the back of the hall, started giggling over Greflinger's bawdy songs, couldn't stop, tried desperately to hold it in, sputtered, tittered, whimpered internally, screamed as though frantic, and all so infectiously that the gathering was carried away by Marthe Elsabe Marie. Harsdörffer laughed so hard that he swallowed the wrong way and his publisher had to slap him on the back. Even from the impassive Schütz the three-part offering wrung a smile. Emanating from Lauremberg, the news was spread about by Schneuber that the giggling Marie had wet both her legs. More laughter. (I saw Scheffler blush.) Only the pious Gerhardt found his judgment confirmed. "What did I tell you? Fit only for the gutter! The stinking gutter!"

Then, after sending the maids into the kitchen with a glance backed up by a gesture, Simon Dach called on Andreas Gryphius to read from his tragedy *Leo Armenius*. (And under his breath he asked Schütz to forgive the assemblage for their childish foolery.)

The moment Gryphius took his seat, the company fell silent. At first he stared at the roof beams. Then in a powerful voice Gryf—as Hofmannswaldau, the systematically antagonistic friend of his youth, called him—launched into his introductory remarks: "At a time when our fatherland lies buried beneath its ashes, transformed into a theater of vanity, I have been at pains, in the present tragedy, to set

before us the transience of human affairs. . . ."
He then announced that his *Leo Armenius* was
to be dedicated to his gracious patron the merchant Wilhelm Schlegel, there present, because
he had written the play while traveling with
Schlegel and could not have done so without
his encouragement. Next he briefly outlined the
plot, named Constantinople as the scene of General Michael Balbus's conspiracy against the
Emperor Leo Armenius, and assured the assembled semicircle that it took more than the rabid
overturning of the old order to create a new one.

Only then did Gryphius, giving weight to
every word but evidently going on for several
manuscript pages too many—quite a few members of the audience, and not only the youngsters but Weckherlin and Lauremberg as well,
fell asleep—read the expository passage beginning with Balbus's conspiratorial harangue: "The
blood that you have risked for throne and crown"
interspersed with the cries of the conspirators,
"His deeds upon his head! The day is dawning,"
and ending with Crambe's oath: "Your sword.
We vow To turn the prince's awesome power to
lightest dust. . . ."

He continued with the arrest scene, larded
with exclamations such as "Heaven help us!
What is this!"—which the bound general concludes with the scornful words, "Stood I in
flaming brimstone, yet would I proclaim: This
is the meed of virtue, this the hero's thanks. . . ."

As an intermezzo Gryphius read the courtiers' strictly constructed three-part statement of the benefits and dangers of the human tongue, the first member or thesis being "Man's very life depends upon his tongue," followed by the antithesis, "Man's death depends on the tongue of every man," while the choral edifice is completed by the third member: "Thy life, O man, and death depend upon thy tongue. . . ."

After the much too verbosely dragged-out trial scene—"Take him to prison; keep an eye on door and locks"—and the Emperor Leo's impassioned monologue passing sentence on the conspirator—"On all the round of earth no drama is so great As when who plays with fire to ashes is reduced'—Gryphius proceeded at long last to the final scene, if not of the play, then at least of his reading.

The dialogue between the Emperor Leo and the Empress Theodosia made a fit ending, for thanks to the empress's eloquent plea that Balbus should not go to the stake until after the holy feast of the Nativity—"Justice has taken its course, let it be mercy's turn"—she succeeds in softening the emperor's grim resolve—"Heaven will bless the head that punishes grim vice"—just a little. "Oh, do not execute stern judgment on the feast day. To God and me, I know, you'll not deny such favor."

Gryphius, who had plenty of breath in reserve and whose mighty voice still filled the hall, would gladly have carried on with the Chorus of Courtiers—"O everlasting vanity, thou mover of all things"—but Dach (with a hand on the reader's shoulder) bade him let well enough alone. The listeners, he said, had heard enough to form an ample picture. He, at all events, felt as though buried beneath an avalanche of words.

Again the assembly sat silent. The light that had piled up outside seeped in through the open windows. Czepko, seated to one side, was watching a butterfly. So much summer after such somber scenes.

Old Weckherlin, who had been awakened from his slumbers by the lively argument and counterargument of the last scene, was first to ask for the floor. Only a misunderstanding could have made him so bold. He praised the author and the end of his play. How gratifying that order should have been maintained and that attempted crime should have met with royal mercy. He hoped that in like manner God would come to the help of poor England, where Cromwell was conducting himself like Balbus in the play. One could not help worrying day and night about the king's safety.

The order-loving secretary of state was rudely corrected by Magister Buchner. The lines they had heard, said Buchner, must make the coming catastrophe clear to all; Gryphius's tragedy was great, and unique in Germany, because it did not in the traditional manner assign guilt onesidedly, but on every side deplored man's frailty and weakness, his vain attempts to do good, since present tyranny was always superseded by new tyranny. Buchner had special praise for the three-part tongue metaphor spoken by the Chorus of Courtiers and called attention to its learned emblematization of the long-tongued purple snail, already mentioned by Aristotle. Then, however, the magister, as though acquitting himself of a duty, expressed mild misgivings about some of the rhymes.

Harsdörffer, speaking as a patriot, criticized the foreign subject matter of the play. It was incumbent, he declared, upon an author with such command of the language as Gryphius had to lend his word-compelling powers to German tragedy, and to it alone.

The scene of action was of no account, said Logau, only the making mattered. And that he must condemn. Such was the welter of words that they drowned in a purple broth, or stabbed one another to death, though the author's intent was manifestly to indict the royal purple and condemn the eternal warfare of the princes. Gryphius's reason advocated order, but his logorrhea wallowed in insurrection.

Partly to state his opinion, but still more in defense of his friend, Hofmannswaldau observed: Yes, Gryf was like that, in love with chaos; his words were in such conflict with one another that they were always turning gray misery to splendor and golden sunlight into darkest gloom; by the power of his words, he laid bare his weakness. But, then, if like Logau he were poorer in language, he could easily make three plays out of one scene.

True enough, Logau replied, he lacked Gryphius's palette, he didn't write with a brush.

Nor with a pen, Hofmannswaldau retorted. More with a stylus.

The contest of wits might have continued and entertained the company for some time, if not for Heinrich Schütz, who suddenly stood up and spoke over the heads of the poets. Yes, he said, he had heard it all. Beginning with the poems, then the speech divided into scenes and apportioned according to roles. First, he would like to praise the clear and beautifully denuded verses of the young medical student, whose name had unfortunately escaped him. If, as he had just heard, the student's name was indeed Johann Scheffler, he would make a note of it. On first hearing, he thought he would be able to compose an eight-part a cappella antiphonal setting for the distich about the rose, or else perhaps for the epigram on essence and accident, which he read: "Become essential, man! When the world fails at last, Accident falls away But Essence, that stands fast." Such words had breath. And if it did not seem presumptuous, he would say that insight such as this was otherwise to be found only in the Holy Scriptures.

But now to the others. Unfortunately, young Birken's verses had passed him by; he would have to read them over; only another reading would show whether there was as much sense as sound in them. Further, he would not deny that, if nothing else, Master Greflinger's ribald songs, the like of which were known to him from his cousin Albert's collection of arias and at which, in view of all the sacrilege rampant throughout the fatherland, he could not take moral umbrage, had a quality conducive to the composition of madrigals. Few German poets, as he knew to his misfortune, mastered that art. How he envied Monteverdi, for whom Guarini had written the loveliest pieces, as had Marino. In the hope of being favored with such texts, he wished to encourage the young man to cultivate the German madrigal, as the late lamented Opitz had attempted to do. Such free-flowing verse, bound by no regular stanza form, could be merry, plaintive, argumentative, even playfully, wildly nonsensical, provided it had breath and left room for the music.

He regretted to say that he found no such room in the dramatic scenes he had heard. Highly as he esteemed the harsh earnestness of Master Gryphius's sonnets, staunchly as he seconded the author's castigation of the vanity of this world, and for all the enduring beauty he perceived in what had just been read, he, as a composer, could find no room among the many, all too many words. No room for a tranquil gesture to unfold. In such a crush no cry of grief could ring out or find an echo. True, everything was said as compactly as could be, but one sharp contour canceled out the next, and the outcome was an overcrowded void. For all the stormy onslaught of words, no movement resulted. To set such a drama to music, one would have to unleash a war of flies. Alas, alas! How fortunate Monteverdi had been to have Maestro Rinuccini at hand with tractable libretti. God bless any poet capable of providing him, Schütz, with a text as beautiful as Arianna's lament. Or something on the order of Tancredi's battle with Clorinda, set so ravishingly to music after the words of Tasso.

But that would be asking too much. He must content himself with less. When the fatherland was laid low, poetry could hardly be expected to flower.

These words were followed not so much by silence as by consternation. Gryphius sat as though thunderstruck. And I, too, felt the blow, as did many others. Gerhardt in particular was galled that only the will-o'-the-wispish Scheffler and the bawdy Greflinger should have been applauded. Already he was on his feet, prepared to attack. He was not at a loss for an answer. He knew what sort of music the word needed. He would show this friend of the Italians, this lover of all that was foreign, this Signor Henrico Sagittario. He would tell him in plain German. He wouldn't mince words. . . .

But Gerhardt was not given leave just yet. Neither Rist nor Zesen, both of whom were perishing to answer, obtained permission. (Nor did I, full as I was of ready words.) Taking a sign from the landlady at the door as an excuse, Simon Dach adjourned the session. Before quarreling, he suggested, they should spoon up their noonday soup in peace.

While the gentlemen were rising from their chairs, Harsdörffer inquired whether Gelnhausen was back, for, so he said, he missed Stoffel.

12

Tasty and fatless. The bacon rind had already done service the day before. A soup that sated but briefly, yet hoped to be long remembered. Barley grits seasoned with chervil. Accompanied by short rations of black bread. Not enough to fill the youngsters' bellies. Greflinger grumbled. Hofmannswaldau, who only the day before had been moved by the meager fare to praise the simple life, observed that simplicity could be overdone. Then he pushed his half-filled bowl over to young Birken. Spoon in soup, Gryphius stirred up thoughts that expanded Silesian hunger into cosmic hunger. Logau joked tersely and testily about the contemporary art of stretching soup. Czepko kept silence over his spoon. Others (Moscherosch, Weckherlin) had stayed away or (like Buchner) had gone to their rooms with their steaming bowls. (Later on, Schneuber circulated the rumor that he had seen one of the maids—Elsabe—following the magister with some extra food wrapped in a cloth.)

As for Schütz, he remained at the table plying his spoon while his cousin Albert entertained him with stories of better days. In the mid-thirties both men had enjoyed King Christian's favor at the court of Copenhagen. Sagittario was heard laughing.

When Harsdörffer, who had been chosen to say grace on this occasion, remarked that few words were needed, since the chervil soup must surely be taken as penance enough, Simon Dach reminded him that a war was still in progress, but, on the other hand, he and the merchant Schlegel and a few of the publishers were going to explore Telgte and would no doubt come back with something they could get their teeth into for supper.

Not even the rats, cried Lauremberg, were finding anything in Telgte. The town was gutted and boarded up, only a sprinkling of inhabitants were left. The gates were barely guarded, and the streets were deserted, except for stray dogs. He and Schneuber had gone there that morning, prepared to pay ready money for a couple of chickens. There was nothing left to cackle in Telgte.

Strange that the pious Gerhardt should have got so worked up. They should have made more careful preparations. Dach, who had done the inviting, should have made sure such strict necessities as bacon and beans were available; after all, he enjoyed his prince's favor. Couldn't a little something have been diverted from his Calvinist larder? He, Gerhardt, asked for no more than the basic needs of every Christian. And moreover, if a guest such as the Saxon court *Kapellmeister* deigned to visit with mere writers of strophic songs, he was entitled to expect better fare.

To this Dach replied: Yes, he deserved to be chided. But he would tolerate no aspersions on his prince's religion. Were the Brandenburg Edicts of Tolerance unknown to Gerhardt?

To them, said Gerhardt, he would not bow. (And much later, as deacon of the Church of St. Nicholas in Berlin, he was to demonstrate his sectarian zeal to the point of being relieved of his office.)

How fortunate that there was still plenty of Rhenish brown beer. Rist made conciliatory gestures. As a Wittenberg authority, Buchner called his former students to order. And when the landlady gave the company hope that Gelnhausen would bring something substantial back with him from Münster, the poets dropped the soup controversy and sank their teeth into phrases and sentences: easily satisfied word-ruminants, finding, if need be, satiety in self-quotation.

Though Schütz's criticism did not prevent Gryphius, however deeply distressed only a moment before, from brushing in the somber scenes of several new tragedies for the benefit of a quickly gathered group of listeners, Schütz's praise had made the Breslau student's manuscripts interesting to several publishers, and young Scheffler did not see how he could decline their offers. Endter of Nuremberg held out the lure of a position as medical officer in that town, and Elzevihr suggested the possibility of a return to Leiden for further study, for he could tell by listening to the student where he—like the young Gryphius in his time—had broadened his mind.

But Scheffler stood firm. He would have to ask counsel elsewhere. (And that no doubt is why I later saw him hurrying once again through the Ems Gate to Telgte, there to kneel, surrounded by the usual old women, before the wooden Pietà. . . .)

Logau and Harsdörffer, at the other end of the long table, asked what had driven Gelnhausen to Münster so early in the morning, and landlady Libuschka spoke from behind her hand as though revealing a secret. Stoffel, she said, had been summoned to the imperial chancellery. Rebellion was not confined to the Weimar troops, and there had also been a mutiny among the Bavarians, who had made their separate peace with the Swedes. General Werth of the cavalry had gone over to the emperor and was trying to breathe new life into the war. His men were a merry crew—she knew them well. She had taken two officers from his regiments as husbands and bed companions, though not for very long. Libuschka then explained why she had given Wallenstein's regiments a wide berth and lost herself in anecdotes about harumscarum campaigns, in the course of which it became known that three years before she had invaded Holstein with Gallas's troops and taken her cut at the pillage of Wedel—how fortunate that Rist was emoting somewhere else. Then she spoke of earlier times, how in her middle twenties, still in the bloom of her youth, in breeches and on horseback, she had served under Tilly and—at the Battle of Lutter—taken a Danish captain prisoner. He would surely, being a nobleman, have made her a countess if the changing fortunes of war had not . . .

It goes without saying that Libuschka had an audience. She knew more than many of the poets about the ups and downs of the contending powers. The course of the war, she said, was decided not by diplomacy, but by the problem of finding winter quarters.

Her stories made them forget Stoffel's mission. As long as she was talking, spreading herself with leaps of time over three decades, even old Weckherlin was eager to hear the Battle of Wimpfen, the Protestant disaster of his youth, described as seen from both banks of the Neckar, and the miracle that favored the Spaniards—the apparition of a white-clad Virgin Mary—accounted for. According to the landlady, a cloud created by exploding ammunition had blown over the battlefield and admitted of Catholic interpretations.

Only when Moscherosch and Rist took turns in reading the appeal of the poets to the princes, which they had drafted in collaboration with Harsdörffer and Hofmannswaldau, but which Dach had not wished them to read that morning, did the company lose interest in the landlady and become inflamed by the fatherland's distress. That, after all, was the reason for their meeting. To make themselves heard. They could at least muster words, if not regiments.

Because Rist was the first to read, the appeal began with a word of fear: "Germany, the most glorious empire in the world, is now bled white, devastated and despoiled. That is the truth. For nigh on thirty years God has visited cruel Mars, accursed war, that most frightful punishment and plague, upon unrepentant Germany for the monstrous wickedness of its innumerable sins. That is the truth! Today the hard-pressed fatherland, lying at its last gasp, yearns to be blessed once more with noblest peace. Wherefore at Telgte, which according to an old interpretation means 'young oak tree,' the poets here assembled have resolved to communicate their views to the German and foreign princes and establish them as the truth. . . ."

Then Moscherosch listed the heads of the parties. First the emperor, then the electors were named in the old order (without Bavaria, but including the Palatinate), with all the respect that Hofmannswaldau's elegant pen had been able to formulate. Then the foreign crowns were invoked, and immediately thereafter, the whole lot of them, of whatever denomination, German, French, and Swedish, were castigated, for the German rulers had opened up the fatherland to foreign hordes, while the foreigners had chosen Germany as their battlefield, so that it now lay dismembered and unrecognizable, all loyalty lost with the old order and all beauty destroyed. The poets alone, so said the appeal, still knew what deserved the name of German. With many "ardent sighs and tears" they had knitted the German language as the last bond; they were the other, the true Germany.

After that (again by Rist and Moscherosch) various demands were lined up, including reinforcement of the Estates, retention by the empire of Pomerania and Alsace, reinstatement of the Palatinate as an independent electorate, restoration of the elective kingdom of Bohemia, and—it goes without saying—religious freedom for all denominations, including the Calvinists. (The Strassburg contingent had made this a condition of their adherence.)

Though at first this manifesto—which was read loudly and emphatically, paragraph by paragraph—aroused enthusiasm, voices were soon heard wishing its arrogance lessened, its demands curtailed, and its practical implications clarified. As was to be expected, Gerhardt took exception to the special mention of the Calvinists. Buchner (now returned from his room) criticized (with a glance at Schütz) the over-sharp condemnation of Saxony. Such "scribbling," said Weckherlin, would neither move

Maximilian to take a single step against the Spaniards, nor spur the landgravine of Hesse against the Swedes. As for the Palatinate, it was gone forever. Logau then declared, tongue in cheek, that once the French cardinal received their epistle, he would abandon all spoils and evacuate Alsace and Breisach forthwith, while one could fancy Oxenstierna, in response to so touchingly German an appeal, losing all interest in Pomerania, including the island of Rügen.

At that Greflinger was fired to indignation. Why was the old slyboots so down on the Swedes? If the heroic Gustavus Adolphus hadn't shipped across the Baltic, even Hamburg would have become Papist. And if Saxony and Brandenburg hadn't time and again hung back like cowards, they might, in league with the Swedes, have advanced to the Danube and beyond. And if Wrangel's cavalry hadn't visited Bavaria the year before, his own hometown of Regensburg would have been closed to him forever.

The Swedes and no one else, cried Lauremberg, had thrown Wallenstein out of Mecklenburg. Hear! cried the Silesians; who, if not the Swedes, would defend them against Rome? For all the hardship of the occupation, there was reason to be grateful. All attacks on the Swedish crown would have to be deleted. Intimidated, young Scheffler sat silent. When Schneuber argued that in that case the French must also be spared, because France had crucially weakened Spain, Zesen said what Rist had been wanting to say: then their document would not be a protest, but only a statement of the usual helplessness. No need to trumpet that. That's not what they had met for. So why were they sitting there?

Heinrich Schütz, who had attended the debate as though absent, answered the question: For the sake of the written words, which poets alone had the power to write in accordance with the dictates of art. And also to wrest from helplessness—he knew it well—a faint "and yet."

With that we could agree. Quickly, as though to take advantage of the brief moment of peace, Simon Dach said that he liked the text, even if it could not be used; that Master Schütz, ordinarily so severe, had only said mildly what everyone knew—that poets were without power, except to write true if useless words. Let them, he recommended, sleep on the appeal; overnight, perhaps, they would arrive at a more propitious version. Then he called the assembly into the great hall for a new disputation. For there, he announced, Gerhardt would at last reply to the world-famous guest.

13

The chervil soup with barley grits may have appeased previously envenomed spirits, or perhaps the appeal to the princes had drained the poets; they sat listlessly in the semicircle as Gerhardt, in a tone of moderation, delivered his speech against the Dresden *Kapellmeister*.

Heinrich Schütz's opinion that German poetry was lacking in breath and clogged with verbiage, that the crush of words left no room for music to unfold with gentle or agitated gestures—this bad mark, with the explanatory gloss that the war had no doubt caused the garden of poetry to wither, remained in force, for, when called on by Dach, Gerhardt spoke in generalities. The guest, he said, looked at everything from the vantage point of his high art; in taking so lofty a view, he lost sight of the simple word, which should serve God before it bowed to art. Wherefore true faith demanded songs that would stand as a barrier to all temptation. Such songs were made for plain people, the congregation should be able to sing them without difficulty. They should, to be precise, have many stanzas, so that from stanza to stanza the singing Christian might soar above his weakness, fortify his faith, and find consolation in evil times. Schütz, said Gerhardt, had scorned to provide poor sinners with the kind of hymns they needed. Even Becker's *Psalter,* as he had heard said in many places, was too convoluted for the church congregations. He, Gerhardt, therefore preferred to lean on his friend Johann Crüger, who as a cantor knew how to work with strophic songs. For Crüger, art was not a lonely tower. He did not cherish the brilliant orchestras of the princes, but set store by the cares of the common man. Along with other, not necessarily world-famous, composers, he was quite content to serve the daily needs of the Christian congregations and compose music for such strophic hymns as the too-soon-departed Fleming's "I leave to his good pleasure," or the revered Johann Rist's "O Ewigkeit, du Donnerwort" ("Eternity, thou word of fear"), or our amiable Simon Dach's "Oh, how blessed are ye saints together," or the recently abused but truly eloquent Gryphius's "The glory of this earth must turn to dust and ashes," or the stanzas that he, Gerhardt, had written in utter devotion to the Lord: "Awake, my heart, and sing," or the more recent "O world behold thy life, upon the Cross doth hang," or "Now all give thanks and praise," or what he had written right here in his room at Telgte: "Thank God, it hath resounded, the blessed voice of joy and peace, Murder's reign is bounded, and spear and sword at last may cease. . . ."

Like a good Saxon, Gerhardt recited every one of the six stanzas, the fourth of which— "and strew fresh seed upon the once so verdant fields, now turned to thicket or parched and barren heath"—found simple words for the state of the fatherland. The assembly was grateful to him. Rist humbly thanked him. Once again young Scheffler was in tears. Gryphius stood up, went over to Gerhardt, and grandly threw his arms around him. After that the general mood was one of thoughtfulness. Schütz sat as though under a bell jar. Albert a prey to inner distress. Dach blew his nose loudly, several times.

Then, speaking into the once more erupting silence, Logau said he wished only to observe that pious hymns, such as those diligently penned for the churches by many here present, were no fit subject for literary discussion. A very different matter, in his opinion, was the high art of Master Schütz, which could not concern itself with the common strophic hymn, because its towering eminence placed it beyond the daily needs of the common man, and yet, though over the heads of the congregations, it redounded solely to the praise of God. Furthermore, said Logau, what Master Schütz had said about the breathless language of the German poets warranted careful consideration. He, in any event, thanked the composer for his lesson.

Czepko and Hofmannswaldau voiced their agreement, Rist and again Gerhardt wished to express a contrary opinion, Gryphius threatened violent eruption, and Buchner, after overlong silence, was pregnant with a long speech. A dispute might well have arisen, especially since Dach seemed irresolute, as though considering himself defenseless before the threatened upsurge of eloquence; but then, unexpectedly (and without being asked), Schütz spoke again.

Seated, he spoke softly, apologizing for having been the occasion of so much misunderstanding. Only his excessive desire for dispassionate yet moving texts had been to blame. He therefore felt obliged to explain once again what sort of language could serve as a handmaiden to music.

Only then did he stand up and, illustrating his thought with the example of his Passion music *The Seven Words on the Cross*, explained what he as a musician demanded of a text— what sustained measures it must admit of, what heightening leave room for. How the gesture implicit in the word must expand in song. To what ecstatic heights words of deep sorrow might rise. Finally, with his still mellifluous old man's voice, he sang the passage about Mary and the apostle: "Woman, woman, behold thy son. . . . John, John, behold thy mother. . . ." Then he sat down again and, seated, once more startling the assembly, proclaimed, first in Latin—*"Ut sol inter planetas . . ."*—and then in German, the motto of Henrico Sagittario: "As the sun amidst the planets, so let music shine amidst the liberal arts."

Still pleased (or horrified) at the moving song, Dach had not noticed, or had pretended not to notice, this new display of arrogance. In any event, he called for more readings without transition: first Zesen, then Harsdörffer and Logau, and last, Johann Rist. Those called were successively willing. Only Rist warned his listeners that he would be obliged to read from a bungled first draft. Each reading was followed by pertinent discussion, which stuck close to the text and no longer, except for the usual excursions into morality, lost itself in theoretical mazes. Sometimes one, sometimes another left the room, either to pass water, or to run into Telgte, or to throw dice with the remaining musketeers in the sunshine outside the stable. (When Weckherlin brought in a complaint next day that money had been stolen from his room, Greflinger was suspected at first, because Schneuber had seen him playing dice.)

Philipp Zesen—The Well-phrasing One, as he was named the following year as a new and soon-to-be-ennobled member of the Fruit-bearing Society—that restless, high-strung, truly youthful man, forever anticipating his innovations with explanatory verbiage, and at all times consumed by several internal fires that stole one another's air, spoke at first chaotically, neglecting to name the subject—corpses drifting in the Ems—of the "terrifying image" that would have to be incorporated into his script if love was to find its appropriate conclusion. Then he collected himself on the stool beside the thistle and read from a pastoral novel already published in Holland, in which a young German by the name of Markhold courts the Venetian Rosamunde in vain, because he, a Lutheran, cannot marry a Catholic unless he promises to have any prospective daughters brought up within the church.

This conflict, which had considerable actuality and still more future, held the company's interest, though the book was known to most of those present, and Zesen's newfangled spelling had already provoked several hostile pamphlets (and first of all a polemic by Rist).

Though Harsdörffer and Birken defended the innovator and intrepid word-builder and Hofmannswaldau praised the gallant flow of the narrative, nevertheless the Adriatic Rosemunde's swoons, her frequent "unwellness"— "Her half-open eyes, her bloodless lips, her silenced tongue, her pallid cheeks, her livid, motionless hands"—provoked disturbing laughter from Rist and others (Lauremberg and Moscherosch) during the reading, and joyous parodies during the discussion period.

Zesen looked as though he were being whipped. He scarcely heard Logau cry out: "You can't deny his courage!" When Buchner finally attempted to check his former student's emotional overflow with cool, authoritative, Opitz-involving discourse, Zesen took refuge in a violent nosebleed. How much of it the gaunt man had. It spurted over his round white collar. It dripped into his still-open book. Dach broke off the discussion. Someone (Czepko or the publisher Elzevihr) helped Zesen to the back of the room and made him lie down on the cool floor, where the bleeding soon stopped.

By then Harsdörffer was sitting beside the thistle. The Playful One, as he was known in the Fruit-bearing Society. An always relaxed, self-assured gentleman with a feeling for novelty, who saw himself more as a learned mentor to talented young men and—exclusively in the interest of Nuremberg—as a patrician statesman, then as an inspired poet. Thus, to the general satisfaction, he read some of his riddles, and the company found entertainment in trying to solve them. By turns a featherbed, a man's shadow, an icicle, the malignant and succulent crab,* and, finally, a dead child in the womb were artfully concealed within a quatrain. Harsdörffer's jocose delivery somewhat diminished the effect.

After much praise, in which Gryphius joined, Birken inquired cautiously, as though asking his mentor for advice, whether it was seemly to couch a child that had died in the womb in so light-footed a verse form.

After qualifying Birken's question as non-

*German *Krebs* = both "cancer" and "crab."—TRANS.

sense, citing and then confuting criticisms from Rist and Gerhardt which had not even been uttered, Buchner, magister of letters, declared that a riddle had just as much right to be cheerful as to be pregnant with a tragic solution; of course, he added, this laconic construct could claim to be nothing more than a minor art form, but it was quite appropriate to the Pegnitz Shepherds.

By then the country nobleman who, though impoverished, had nevertheless found security as administrator of the Duke of Brieg's properties had taken his place on the stool and, by spitting two of his three hand-sized sheets of paper on its thorns, given the plant a collateral, ironic meaning. The Belittler was his title in the Fruit-bearing Society. And Logau spoke with his trusted succinctness. Sarcastically and too irreverently for some of the listeners' taste, he said more in two lines than a long dissertation could have unsaid. About the religions, for instance: "Lutheran, Papist, Calvinist—these faiths exist all three. But who can tell us just what is Christianity?" Or in view of the coming peace: "When peace is made amid such devastation, Hangmen and juris-consults will dominate the nation."

After two poems of some length, one being the monologue of a wartime dog, Logau concluded with a couplet dealing with feminine fashion, which he wished expressly to dedicate to landlady Libuschka's maids: "Womenfolk are so confiding, Wear their dresses cut so low,

That the rolling hills give tiding Of the sultry warmth below."

After Hofmannswaldau and Weckherlin, even Gryphius showed approval. As did Buchner by his silence. Someone thought he had detected a smile on Schütz's face. Rist publicly contemplated trying the couplet about the religions on his Wedel congregation when next he addressed them from the pulpit. When—the others had a good idea why—the pious Gerhardt raised his hand, Dach overlooked it and answered the overlooked would-be questioner by saying that if anyone were to take umbrage at Logau's outspokenness, he would shut him up that night with the three maids, for he knew of certain gentlemen who had descended from the hills to the lowlands in their company.

While the poets cast mocking glances at one another, while Greflinger whistled a tune, while Birken smiled with moist lips, Schneuber waxed offensive under his breath, and Lauremberg inquired what had become of young Scheffler. Buchner said: Oh, well, haste was in order. With time so short, only brief subsidiary action was possible.

Meanwhile, amid laughter, the "Elbe Swan" had occupied the stool between Dach and the thistle. Such was the name sometimes given to Johann Rist, by way of allusion to Opitz, the "Bober Swan," by the friends with whom Rist, as a member of the Fruit-bearing Society, in which he was known as The Valiant One, corresponded. Everything about Rist was imposing, his resounding parsonical word flow, his chamberlainlike entrances, his homespun marshland humor, his gigantic frame always clad in the best broadcloth, his beard, his firm, substantial nose, and even, what with his crafty way of narrowing his left eye, his watery gaze. He had an opinion about everything. Nothing escaped him uncontradicted. Though he wasted his strength in feuds (not only with Zesen), he was nevertheless an industrious writer. Irresolutely at first, he now began to rummage through his papers; then finally he gave himself a jolt and was ready.

Rist informed his audience that, by way of anticipating the peace treaty that was still being negotiated amid the din of battle, he had begun to write a dramatic work to be entitled *Germany Jubilant over the Peace*. In it, a female figure would appear as Truth. "For Truth must proclaim or announce to you certain things that will be dear to the hearts of many, but to many may possibly bring no little sorrow. Therefore, ye Germans, give ear!"

He read a few scenes of the first interlude, in which a war-weary junker, talking with two peasants, deplores their moral depravity. The peasants, he explains, have been bled by the soldiery, and from the soldiery, they have learned the art of bleeding others. Just like the soldiers, they steal, loot, extort, drink, and whore. Consequently, they dread the coming of peace, which may well mean the end of their dissolute life. When in response the peasants Drewes Kikintlag and Beneke Dudeldey praise their merry life as highwaymen and drunkards in pithy Low German—"What's the war to us? Let 'em fight, let 'em bleed, as long as there's plenty to drink at our hostler Peter Langwamme's house"—the nobleman waxes indignant in stilted chancellery German: "May God have mercy, what is this I hear? Would you wretches rather suffer the brutal pressures of war than live in concord, peace, and tranquillity under your lawful authorities?" But the peasants prefer the chaotic wartime conditions to the extortionate taxes they can look forward to once peace breaks out. They fear the old order and its return, disguised as a new order. The war levies imposed by one army or another are not nearly so hard to bear as the future burden of taxation.

Rist read the short scene in which, as though reversing their roles, the officer praises peace while the peasants want to prolong the war, with the skill of an actor holding first one, then another mask over his face. Too bad that only a few could follow the Holstein dialect. After his reading, the author had to translate the pithiest bits for Moscherosch, Harsdörffer, Weckherlin, and the Silesians, and, losing their flavor in the process, they became as flat as the junker's speeches. Consequently, the discussion revolved not so much around the scene from Rist's peace play, as around the general decline of morality.

Everyone knew of dreadful examples: How when Breisach was besieged, homeless children were butchered and eaten. How in places where order had been put to flight, the mob set themselves up as masters. How the most flea-bitten yokels swaggered about in city finery. And everyone knew of highwaymen in Franconia, in Brandenburg, behind every bush. For the tenth time, Schneuber complained of how he had been robbed on his way from Strassburg with Moscherosch. There was talk of evildoers, some already hanged and others still running around loose. Harsh words were devoted to the Swedes and their ruthless foraging expeditions. But while numerous Silesian voices were still chronicling and multiplying gruesome details (the Swedish drink, charred feet), the regimental secretary suddenly (I had been hearing noise—the barking of the tavern mongrels—outside for some time) burst into the room.

Still in his green doublet, still with a feather in his hat, he leapt into the midst of the gentlemen, saluted in the imperial manner, and proclaimed the end of the barley-soup era: no more short rations, for five geese, three suckling pigs, and a fat sheep had come his way. In his passage he had been showered with sausages. If the gentlemen didn't believe him, he declared, they could see all that for themselves. Already his men could be seen turning spits in the courtyard. There would be a feast to which the assembled poets need only contribute Lucullean double rhymes, Epicurean iambi, Bacchanalian epigrams, Dionysian dactyls, and words of Platonic wisdom. For even if it was too soon to celebrate the peace, they could at least celebrate the last gasps of the war. He therefore entreated them to go right out into the court-yard and marvel at the skill with which Stoffel, known from Bohemia to Breisgau, from the Spessart Mountains to the plains of Westphalia as Simplicius, had foraged for German poetry.

They did not go out at once. Dach insisted on order. It was still up to him, he said, whether or not to adjourn the session, and until such time he would countenance further argument and rebuttal. After all, they wouldn't want the Elbe Swan to have sung in vain.

And so for a short period of give and take we prolonged the discussion of Rist's scene and of the moral depravity that had swept the coun-try. Gryphius suggested that if the scene were played before the dull, unthinking public, they would applaud the peasants rather than the junker. Moscherosch praised Rist for having the courage to dramatize the grievous state of the country. But—Czepko asked himself and others—were the peasants not right in fearing the return of the old order? Yes, cried Laurem-berg, but what order could one wish for if not the good, old one?

For fear of giving the argument further fuel with an inquiry into the question of a new and possibly just order, and because the aroma of roast meat was already rising from the court-yard, Simon Dach signaled the increasingly restless gathering that the afternoon session was adjourned. Several poets—and not only the youngsters—hurried out into the open. Others took their time. The last to leave the great hall were Dach, Gerhardt, and Schütz, the last two engaged in quiet conversation, as though reconciled. Only the thistle, in its place beside the empty stool, remained behind. Outside, the goings-on were dithyrambic.

14

The five geese were already lined up on one spit and the three suckling pigs on the second, while the sheep stuffed with sausages was turning on the third. The long table from the tap-room had been moved up to the bushes bordering the outer arm of the Ems, so that it remained untouched by the smoke from the fires that were flaring in the middle of the courtyard. Landlady Libuschka and her maids rushed back and forth between house and courtyard, setting the table. Closer inspection revealed that the tablecloths had formerly done service on an altar. The plates, cups, mugs, and bowls seemed to belong in one of the many Westphalian moated castles. Apart from two-pronged serving forks, there was no other cutlery.

Blowing across the courtyard in the direction

of the stable, the smoke veiled the alders that fringed the inner arm of the Ems and bordered the town, the gables of the Herrenstrasse, and off to one side the parish church. Gelnhausen's musketeers attended the roasting spits. Since they caught the fat dripping from the geese, pigs, and sheep in earthenware bowls, they were able to baste the roasts continually with goose, pork, and mutton fat. From the juniper bushes that covered the Emshagen as far as the fulling mill, the stableboy brought dry fagots, which from time to time made the fires smoke more abundantly. The town of Telgte lay flat-painted behind the animated picture into which the tavern dogs kept moving, sometimes singly, sometimes gathered into a pack. (Later they fought over the bones.)

Meanwhile Gelnhausen's horsemen were busy driving stakes into the ground, on which to stretch patterned canvas—that might have been taken from the tent of a Hessian colonel—over the laid table like a canopy. Garlands were plaited of fresh foliage, and wild roses from the landlady's garden woven into them. Soon garlands were affixed to the stakes of the canopy. The fringes around its edges were twisted into tassels, on which hung bells that later, when a breeze came up, contributed to the festive mood.

Although it was still day and the dusk was taking its time in falling, Gelnhausen brought five heavy silver candlesticks of ecclesiastical origin, still fitted with almost unused candles, from the covered wagon that had been harnessed

121

that morning and had brought the geese and pigs and sheep, altar cloths and canopy. Stoffel then placed the three-armed silver pieces on the table. After several attempts to position them informally, he adopted a military stance as though lining up a company. Off to one side in groups, the poets saw all that; and I kept the record.

When under Gelnhausen's supervision a figure the size of a small boy, cast in bronze and representing Apollo, was brought from the inexhaustible covered wagon, when finally this work of art was placed in the middle of the table (after the candlesticks had once again been moved), Simon Dach felt obliged to do something more than stand dumbfounded, admiring the display with mounting trepidation. Taking aside first the landlady, then Gelnhausen, he asked where and by what right these treasures had been seized, how paid for, or with whose permission borrowed. So much miscellaneous richness—meat linen metal—did not, he said, fall from the trees.

Yes, said Gelnhausen, all that was true, and he also had to admit that the geese, pigs, and sheep came from Catholic houses, but the whole transaction could only be regarded as honorable, for on the occasion of his necessarily secret visit to Münster—and there were incidentals that he was still unable to divulge—several of the delegates to the peace conference had spoken with enthusiasm of the meeting of German poets, which had been bruited about by then.

Monsignor Chigi, the papal nuncio, had commissioned him to ask Harsdörffer to write a personal dedication into his, Chigi's, copy of the *Conversation Plays for Women,* a first edition dated 1641, which he carried with him at all times. Venetian Ambassador Contarini sent greetings to Maestro Sagittario, who was still remembered at St. Mark's, and took the liberty of informing him once again that Master Schütz's return to Venice would at any time call forth not one but many ovations. The Marquis de Sablé had immediately sent a courier to Cardinal Mazarin with the news of the poets' gathering, and would have his palace put in order if the company would do him the honor. Only the Swedish ambassador, newly arrived from Osnabrück, had made eyes like a calf in a thunderstorm on hearing the world-famous names, which were Greek to him, even though the great Oxenstierna was his father. But Count Johann von Nassau, who had been representing the emperor at the conference since Trauttmannsdorff's departure, had been all the more cordial and had hastened to bid Isaak Volmar, a high official at the imperial chancellery, to provide for the well-being of the poets who had traveled so far, and make certain they did not lack for sustenance, refreshment, or loving gifts. And here, sure enough, was a gold ring for Herr Dach, here finely wrought silver cups, and here, and here . . . Whereupon Volmar, equipped with written instructions concerning the forthcoming banquet, had turned Gelnhausen's knowledge of the country to account. He, Gelnhausen, had hurried hither and thither. For indeed he knew Westphalia like the back of his hand. As the once famous huntsman of Soest, he had familiarized himself with every nook and cranny in the triangle formed by Dorsten, Lippstadt, and Coesfeld. Münster itself had been unable to offer much; everything went to the embassies. But the surrounding countryside still had resources. In short: as an imperial agent acting on instructions from Count von Nassau, he had had little difficulty in carrying out the order, for one thing because the region was more Catholic than the Pope ever meant it to be. There was plenty of everything. Only game would be wanting. Would Herr Dach care to see the list? Every single item checked off—wine, cheese, and so on. Was Master Dach displeased?

At first Dach had listened to the report (rounded out with anecdotes about the doings in Münster and adorned with here uncited subordinate clauses invoking members of the ancient pantheon as witnesses) by himself, then accompanied by Logau, Harsdörffer, Rist, and Hofmannswaldau, and finally surrounded by us all. He had listened at first with distrust, then with increasing wonderment, and at the end feeling somewhat flattered. He toyed with the gold ring, which embarrassed him. The silver cups passed from hand to hand. Though Logau (from old habit) might make a barbed remark or two, though there might seem to be a bit of exaggeration in the report, the company were not loath to accept greetings and commendations from persons so highly placed. And when Gelnhausen produced from his courier's bag a copy of the *Conversation Plays for Women*—true enough, a first edition, dated 1641!—the *ex libris* of which identified the owner as Fabio Chigi, the papal nuncio (later Pope Alexander VII), held out the book, and smilingly asked Harsdörffer to write in a dedication at his convenience, everyone was convinced that there could be nothing dishonorable about the forthcoming banquet; even Logau was mute.

Residual doubts—could they as good Lutherans accept these popish gifts?—were dispelled by Dach, who reminded Gryphius, and finally Rist and Gerhardt as well, of the revered Opitz's willingness to serve the Catholic cause, of how as an irenicist in the tradition of the learned Grotius and as a student of the late Lingelsheim, the Bober Swan had at all times advocated freedom of religion and opposed all exclusivity. Ah, if only the peace proved such that Lutherans would dine at one table with Catholics and Catholics with Lutherans and Calvinists. As for himself, in any event, even a Catholic suckling pig made his mouth water.

And then the landlady called out that the meat was ready to carve.

15

At last! cried Greflinger, shaking his black
curls, which tumbled over his shoulders. Rist
and Lauremberg felt certain of having deserved
this roast meat. But Czepko and Logau had
misgivings: what if the Devil had kindled the
three cooking fires? Birken was determined to
do justice to what he had so long gone without.
And he promised the silent Scheffler, whose
eyes were on the maids, that he would. With
wolfish hunger Moscherosch thrust himself
between Harsdörffer and his publisher. When
Gryphius boasted of his spacious stomach,
Hofmannswaldau reminded him of the transience of the palate's joys. Schneuber's arse was
still so sore that even in the presence of such
gastronomic delights he found it hard to sit
down. Old Weckherlin thought he had better

wrap a goose breast in his handkerchief as a provision for hungry times ahead, and he advised Gerhardt to do the same. Looking past Zesen, who was staring spellbound at the cooking fires, Gerhardt threatened to impose moderation on the company when he said grace. But Dach, who had his Albert beside him, said that on this occasion young Birken would pray aloud for all. Albert cast a searching look around him and asked a question of the merchant Schlegel, who passed it on to the publisher Mülbe by way of Elzevihr, but by the time the question had reached Buchner, it had answered itself: Schütz was absent from the table.

How do I know all this? I was sitting in their midst, I was there. It was no secret to me that landlady Libuschka had sent one of her maids to town to recruit wenches for the night. Who was I? Neither Logau nor Gelnhausen. Still others might have been invited—Neumark, for instance, but he stayed in Königsberg; or Tscherning, whose absence was especially deplored by Buchner. Whoever I may have been, I knew that the wine in the casks was sacramental. My ear picked up what the imperial musketeers called out to one another while carving the geese, the pigs, and the sheep. I had seen Schütz—as soon as he had entered the courtyard, caught sight of the preparations, and listened for a moment to Gelnhausen—go back into the house and climb the stairs to his room. I even knew what no one else did, that while the banquet of the German poets was getting

under way at the Bridge Tavern in Telgte, the
Bavarian delegates in Münster were pledging
Alsace to France and obtaining the Palatinate
(plus a promise of the electoral dignity) in
return. Wretched horse trading! I could have
cried, but I laughed, because I was privileged to
be there, to be present while under the Hessian
canopy, in the gathering dusk, the candles in
the Catholic candlestick were lighted and we
clasped our hands. For now Birken, who was
sitting next to Scheffler, stood up, half concealed from me by the child-size Apollo but
equally beautiful, to pronounce an out-and-out
Protestant grace: "May Lord Jesus set us free,
In the world to flee. . . ." Then, standing in his
place halfway down the table, the outer Ems
behind him and before him the town, darkened
against the sky—Dach spoke again to them all,
though the carved meat was already steaming
in the seignorial porcelain. Possibly because
Birken's grace had been too somber and unworldly—"Let us, while we are living, mortify
our flesh"—Dach, whose Christianity was of a
more practical nature, wished to provide earthly
encouragement. If even the spirit did not live
by the spirit alone, it was fitting, he said, that a
proper morsel should fall to the lot of poor
poets, those forever hungry onlookers. Consequently, he would not trouble Gelnhausen—to
whom thanks—with further questions about
the whence, but let well enough alone. And in
the hope that God's blessing rested on everything that the table bore so superabundantly,

he bade his friends do well by their far from spoiled palates. And might the present banquet provide an ample foretaste of the peace to come!

They fell to. With both hands. With elbows devoutly propped. With Silesian, Franconian, Elbian, Brandenburgian, Alemannic hunger. Similarly the horsemen, the musketeers, the tavern mongrels, the stableboy, the maids, and the town wenches. They attacked the geese, the pigs, and the sheep. Half of what the sheep had had inside it, the blood sausages and liver sausages, had been put on the table, while half had stayed with the cooks. Into the juice, which dripped from rounded beards, pointed beards, and twirled mustaches and stood fatty in the dishes, they dipped freshly baked white bread. How crisply the skin of the suckling pigs crackled. The juniper fagots had lent their savor to the meat, especially to the mutton.

Only the landlady and Gelnhausen kept moving restlessly back and forth. They continued to serve up the food—millet steamed in milk with raisins, bowls full of crystallized ginger, sweet pickles, plum butter, great jugs of red wine, dry goat cheese, and lastly the sheep's head, which had been prepared in the kitchen. Into the mouth Libuschka had wedged a large beet; she had encased the neck in a gentlemanly white collar, and with a crown of marsh marigolds transformed the head into a crowned sheep's head. As Courage carried it in, her queenly bearing gave further dignity to the head she was dishing up.

129

That admitted of jokes. The sheep's head demanded comparisons. Homage was paid to it in iambi and trochees, in trisyllabic feet, Buchnerian dactyls, and alexandrines, with metathesis, alliteration, internal rhymes, and nimble improvisations. Assuming the role of a betrayed sheep, Greflinger bewailed the loss of his faithless Flora; the others resorted to political allusions.

"Nor eagle proud nor lion, Adorns the German blazon, But the good submissive sheep" was Logau's contribution. Moscherosch made the emblematic beast of the Germans "converse in courtly Spanish wise." Gryphius, who was shoveling the food in as though determined to engulf the world, desisted from the forepaw of a piglet for the time it took to rhyme: "The sheep that bleats for peace forever Will get it from the butcher's cleaver."

Augustus Buchner, magister of letters, put up with hasty rhymes, pretended not to hear Zesen's "Three four seven eight eleven, All good sheep will go to heaven," and only remarked on how lucky it was that the stern Schütz had been spared such tidbits. . . . In response to which the startled Dach desisted from the goose leg he had coated with plum butter, looked around at the likewise startled company, and asked his Albert to go quickly and see to their guest.

The cathedral organist found the old man in his room, lying coatless on his bed. Raising himself a little, Schütz said it was kind of them to notice his absence, but he would like to rest another little while. He had many new impressions to think over. The realization, for example, that cutting wit, such as Logau's, was not conducive to music. Yes indeed. He was ready to believe that a merry mood prevailed down there in the courtyard. The merriment rose up to his room polyphonically, making a mockery of thoughts such as this: if, as he believed, reason was prejudicial to music, if, in other words, the writing of music was at cross-purposes with the rational writing of words, how, then, was it possible that Logau should nevertheless, with cool, unclouded mind, achieve beauty? Cousin Albert might well be inclined to smile at such hairsplitting and call him a lawyer manqué. Ah, yes, if only he had persevered in his study of the law, before music had taken up all his attention. But his period of apprenticeship in Marburg had sharpened his wits, which still came in handy. Given a little time, he could see through the finest fabric of lies. Some little thread was always missing. Now take that ruffian Stoffel, who, to be sure, spun more amusingly than some of the visiting poets: the world of lies he concocted had a logic of its own. What? Was Cousin Albert still taken in? In that case he would not disturb his sweet simplicity. Yes, yes, he would be down after a while for a glass of something. Sooner or later. No need to worry. His cousin should just go and make merry.

Only when Albert was halfway through the door did Schütz speak briefly of his accumulated worries. He called his circumstances in

Dresden wretched. On the one hand, he regarded his return to Weissenfels as desirable; on the other, he was in a hurry to go to Hamburg and beyond to Glückstadt. There he hoped to find a message from the Danish court, an invitation to Copenhagen: operas, ballets, sprightly madrigals. . . . Lauremberg had given him hope. The crown prince was devoted to the arts. In any case he was carrying with him a printed score of the second part of the *Sinphoniae sacrae*, dedicated to the prince. Then Schütz lay down again but did not close his eyes.

In the courtyard the news that the Dresden *Kapellmeister* would come down for a while later on was received with relief. Partly because it was not vexation that was keeping the world-famous man away, and partly because the stern guest would still be absent for a time from the poets' merry-to-tumultuous board. We welcomed the prospect of being among ourselves for a while longer.

Greflinger and Schneuber had motioned the landlady's three maids over to the table as well as—with Gelnhausen's encouragement—a few of the wenches from Telgte. Elsabe was sitting on Moscherosch's lap. Someone, presumably old Weckherlin, had foisted two excessively low-cut women on the pious Gerhardt. The dainty and delicate Marie leaned on the student Scheffler with the familiarity of old acquaintance, and the young man was soon heaped with mockery. In which pursuit Lauremberg and Schneuber distinguished themselves. Was Marie substituting for the Blessed Virgin? Was he intending to become a Catholic by mating with her? And suchlike offensive remarks, until Greflinger gave them a piece of his Bavarian mind and showed his fists.

Elsewhere Rist, whose preacher's hand had been exploring one of the town wenches' topography, was insulted by Logau. The Belittler had only wanted to tell The Valiant One that his busy treasure hunting seemed to leave him no free hand for the wine jug. Whereupon Rist, gesticulating with both hands, had waxed loudly bellicose. Logau's wit, he declared, was corrosive because it lacked wholesome humor, and because it lacked wholesome humor it was no better than irony, and because it was ironical it was not German, and because it was not German, it was intrinsically "un-German and anti-German."

This gave rise to a new disputation, during which the maids and wenches were as good as forgotten. The argument over the essence of irony and of humor kept the company too busy to do anything but reach thirstily for the wine jugs. Soon Logau stood alone, for Zesen now joined Rist in denigrating, and in the most literal sense "damning," his belittling view of things, people, and conditions as alien, un-German, Gallic, and, in a word, ironic; for once in agreement, Rist and Zesen termed the usually two-line epigrams of the always insidious Logau mere works of the Devil. Why? Because irony is the work of the Devil. Why of the

Devil? Because it's French and therefore diabolical.

Hofmannswaldau tried to put an end to this all too German quarrel, but his humor hardly served the purpose. Old Weckherlin, freshly returned from England, was amused by the old-country uproar. Fortified with wine but no longer a master of words, Gryphius contributed fiendish laughter. When Moscherosch ventured a word in Logau's favor, remarks were dropped about his name, which couldn't be Moorish and was certainly—by God!—not German in origin. Lauremberg shouted the evil word from ambush. A fist struck the table. Wine sloshed over. Greflinger scented a brawl. Dach had risen to stem this outburst of violence with his thus far respected "That's enough, children!" when out of the darkness Heinrich Schütz came striding across the courtyard and sobered the company.

Although the guest begged the poets not to let him disrupt their conversation, the humor-irony controversy evaporated forthwith. No one had meant any harm. The maids and wenches withdrew to the still-flaming cooking fires. Buchner relinquished the chair intended for Schütz. Dach gave vent to his joy that the guest had finally come—better late than never. Landlady Libuschka wanted to slice him some hot leg of mutton. Gelnhausen poured wine. But Schütz neither ate nor drank. In silence he surveyed the table and then looked out at the fires in the courtyard, around which the musketeers and horsemen had begun their own festivities. One of the musketeers was a passable bagpiper. Two, then three couples were seen dancing before and behind the fire in varying illumination.

After contemplating the bronze Apollo for some time and the silver candlesticks only briefly, Schütz turned to Gelnhausen, who was still standing beside him with a wine jug. And flung the question straight in Stoffel's face: how had one of the horsemen and that musketeer—the one dancing there!—come by their head wounds? He demanded a straight answer and no evasions.

Whereupon all those at the table learned that a bullet had grazed the horseman and a dragoon's saber had wounded the musketeer—only slightly, praise God.

When Schütz questioned further, it was learned that an engagement had occurred between Gelnhausen's imperial troops and a Swedish detachment stationed in Vechta. But they had put the foraging Swedes to flight.

And taken spoils in the process? Schütz persisted.

It then came to light that the Swedes had just slaughtered the geese, pigs, and sheep on the farm of a peasant whom, admittedly, Gelnhausen had been planning to visit. The good man, whom sad to say the Swedes had spitted to his barn door, was an old acquaintance from the days when he, Gelnhausen, had been known throughout the region as the huntsman of Soest. Ah, he and his green doublet with the gold buttons had . . .

Schütz wasn't standing for any digressions. It finally came out that the church silver, the child-size Apollo, the Hessian tent canvas, the castle porcelain, and the altar cloths, not to mention the plum butter, crystallized ginger, sweet pickles, cheese, and white bread, had been found in a covered wagon captured from the Swedes.

As though to keep his report as realistic as possible, Gelnhausen explained how it had been necessary to transfer the cargo, because in trying to get away, the Swedish vehicle had sunk axle-deep into a bog.

Who had given him the order for this robbery?

That, said Gelnhausen, seemed to be roughly the gist of Count von Nassau's instructions as passed on to him by the imperial chancellery. It was not robbery, however, but a military engagement that had resulted in the transfer of the foragers' loot. Exactly as ordered.

What was the precise wording of this imperial order?

The count had sent cordial and courteous greetings and bidden him, Gelnhausen, see to the material needs of the assembled poets.

Did this solicitude necessarily imply loot—that is, as an assortment of roast meat, sausages, two casks of wine, finely wrought bronze, and other luxuries?

In view of yesterday's experience with the fare at the Bridge Tavern, the count's instructions to provide for their material needs could not have been carried out more nutritively. And as for the modest festive setting, had Plato not written . . . ?

As though to leave no area of shadow, Schütz then asked Stoffel, whether, apart from the peasant, other persons had been injured in the disgraceful robbery. And Gelnhausen replied casually that it had all happened so quickly, but as far as he could remember, the rough manners of the Swedes had not agreed with the hired man and the maidservant. And as she lay dying, the peasant woman had worried about her little boy, whom he, Gelnhausen, praise God, had seen running into the nearby woods, so escaping the butchery.

Stoffel went on to say that he knew a story that had had a similar sad beginning in the Spessart Mountains. For that was just what had happened to him as a boy. "Paw and Maw" had perished miserably. But he was still alive. God grant that as much good fortune could come the way of the little Westphalian boy.

The festive board was a picture of desolation. Piles of bones big and little. Puddles of wine. The formerly crowned, now half-eaten sheep's head. The disgust. The burned-down candles. The savagely barking mongrels. The bells on the canopy tinkled in mockery. The general gloom was deepened by the merriment of the horsemen and musketeers; around the fires, with the women, they sang, laughed, and bellowed undismayed. It took a shout from the landlady to silence the bagpiper. Off to one side, Birken vomited. The poets stood in groups.

137

Scheffler was not alone in weeping: Czepko and the merchant Schlegel did likewise. Gerhardt was heard praying under his breath. Still under the influence of wine, Gryphius staggered around the table. Logau assured Buchner that he had suspected skulduggery from the start. (With some difficulty I restrained Zesen from going to the Ems to see corpses drifting.) And Simon Dach stood there like a broken man, breathing heavily. His Albert opened his shirt. Only Schütz kept his composure.

He was still in his armchair by the table. And from his seat he advised the poets to go on with their meeting and dispense with useless lamentations. In the eyes of God, he said, their complicity in the horror was slight. Their undertaking, however, which would benefit the language and help their unfortunate fatherland, remained great and must be carried on. He hoped he had not interfered with it.

Then he stood up and said good-bye—especially to Dach, warmly to Albert, to the others with a gesture. Before setting out, he informed the company that he was leaving early because of his hurry to get to Hamburg and beyond, not because of the shameful incident.

Brief orders were given—Dach sent Greflinger for Schütz's luggage. Then the *Kapellmeister* took Gelnhausen aside, and they walked a few steps together. To judge by his tone, the old man spoke kindly, words of comfort. Once he laughed, then both laughed. When Stoffel went down on his knees before him, Schütz pulled him up. It seems, as Harsdörffer later reported, that he told the regimental secretary never again to put his murderous fictions into practice, but to write them down bravely, for life had given him lessons enough.

Along with the covered wagon, two imperial horsemen escorted Schütz as far as Osnabrück. By torchlight the gentlemen stood in the courtyard. Then Simon Dach summoned the gathering to the taproom, where the long table was again standing as though nothing had happened.

16

"O empty dream, whereon we mortals build . . ." Everything went sour. Horror clouded the mirrors. The meanings of words were reversed. Hope languished beside the silted well. Built on desert sand, no wall stood firm. In all the world nothing endured but mockery. The world's false glitter. The green branch foredoomed to wither. The whited sepulcher. The painted corpse. The plaything of false fortune . . . "What is the life of man, with all its shifts and changes, But a fantasy of time!"

Since the beginning of the war, but more disastrously since young Gryphius's first sonnets, published in Lissa, everything had struck them as hopeless. For all the lusts that swelled their sentence structure, for all the daintiness with which they clipped nature, transforming it into a pastoral rich in grottoes and mazes, for all their facility in devising sonorous words and sound patterns that obliterated more meaning than they communicated, always in the last stanza the earth became a vale of tears. Even the lesser poets found no difficulty in celebrating death as liberation. Avid for honor and fame, they rivaled one another in framing the vanity of human endeavor in sumptuous images. The younger poets were especially quick to dispose of life in their verses. But the older ones as well were so used to taking leave of this earth and its frippery that the valeoftearishness and deathwhereisthystingishness of their industriously (and for modest reward) penned commissions could easily be regarded as fashionable and nothing more; for which reason Logau, who kept a cool head and sided with reason, often poked fun at his colleagues' rhymed yearning for death. And several moderate proponents of the "All is vanity" thesis joined him now and then in looking behind the somber backs of one another's cards and discovering their bright-colored faces.

Accordingly, not only Logau and Weckherlin, but also the shrewd and experienced Hofmannswaldau and Harsdörffer regarded as pure superstition the current belief that the end of the world would soon corroborate the poetic croakings that had been at such pains to bring it about. But the others—and with them the satirists and even the worldly-wise Dach—saw the Day of Judgment within reach, not always, to be sure, but whenever the political horizon, as often happened, darkened, or the commonplace problems of life tangled themselves into a knot—when, after Gelnhausen's confession, for example, the poets' banquet could only be regarded as an orgy of gluttony and their merrymaking was turned to lamentation.

Only Gryphius, the master of gloom, emanated good cheer. This sort of mood was his stock in trade. Serenely he stood firm amid chaos. To his mind, all human order was built on delusion and futility.

Consequently, he laughed. Why all the fuss? Had they ever known a feast that did not automatically drown itself in horror?

For the present, however, the assembled poets could not stop staring into the jaws of hell. That was the pious Gerhardt's hour. Rist, too, was hard at work. Out of Zesen's mouth Satan triumphed in sound patterns. Young Birken's pouting lips drooped pathetically. The more inward-looking Scheffler and Czepko were seen to seek salvation in prayer. All the publishers, especially Mülbe, whose usual occupation was forging plans, foresaw the end of their trade. And Albert recalled lines by his friend Dach:

> See how all life on earth doth pass,
> Now that death's snout obscene
> Is with us drinking from our glass
> And wiping all our dishes clean.

It was only when the poets seated around the table had savored their misery long enough that they began to accuse themselves and one another. Harsdörffer in particular was accused of foisting a highwayman on their company. Just because the fellow was always ready with a quip, said Buchner angrily, the Pegnitz Shepherds had deemed him worthy of a recommendation. Zesen chided Dach for having let the crude vagabond speak at their confidential sessions. Moscherosch, on the other hand, pointed out that they were indebted to the swine for their lodgings. And Hofmannswaldau scoffed that this first, by no means negligible, deception had only made most of them laugh. Once again Gryphius triumphed (though modestly): What did they expect? Everyone wallowed in sin. Everyone was burdened with guilt. Gathered together as they all were in their sinfulness, regardless of station, death alone could make the crooked straight before God.

To Dach's mind this verdict of universal guilt amounted to a universal acquittal. He would have none of it. The present problem, he said, was not to deplore man's innate depravity or to seek out individual culprits, but to assign responsibility. And that he must charge first of all to himself. He, more than anyone else, must acknowledge the guilt. It would never occur to him to turn their disgrace, which was primarily his disgrace, into an amusing story to tell in Königsberg. But as to what they should do now, he, too, was at a loss. Schütz—a pity he'd gone—was right. The meeting must be carried to its conclusion. They couldn't just run away.

When Harsdörffer took all responsibility on himself and offered to leave, no one would hear of it. Buchner said his accusations had been uttered in the heat of anger. If Harsdörffer went, he would go, too.

Might they not, merchant Schlegel suggested, consider holding a court of honor of the kind customary in the Hanseatic towns, and judge Gelnhausen's crime in his presence? Since he, Schlegel, was not of the same station as the poets, he would be willing to serve as judge.

Cries of Yes! A trial! The fellow, cried Zesen, must not be allowed to attend further readings and molest them with his insolent interruptions. Rist protested that the final framing of the poets' appeal for peace, scheduled for the next day, must not take place in the presence of a common tramp, and Buchner added that, much as the scoundrel might have picked up here and there, he was utterly uneducated.

All seemed to favor the court of honor. When Logau asked whether the verdict, which could not be in doubt, should be pronounced now or later, and who was prepared to seek out Stoffel among his musketeers and summon him into court, no one volunteered. When Lauremberg cried out that since Greflinger felt happiest in the baggy breeches of a soldier, he was the man to do it, it became evident that Greflinger was absent.

Schneuber's instant suspicion: He's in league with Gelnhausen. But when Zesen went further in his imputations—suggesting that "they" must be planning further "injury to the German poets"—Dach made it clear that he had never had an ear for calumny. He himself would go. It was his duty, and his alone, to summon Gelnhausen.

This Albert and Gerhardt would not countenance. It would be dangerous, said Weckherlin, to provoke the drunken imperials at such an hour. And after the usual argument, Moscherosch's suggestion of calling the landlady was also rejected. In response to Rist's shout that they should convict the fellow *in absentia,* Hofmannswaldau retorted that that sort of trial was not to his liking, and if that was what they wanted, they could convict him, too.

Once again general perplexity. All sat silent around the long table. Only Gryphius chose to be amused at the renewed upsurge of lamentation. The only remedy for life, said he, was death.

At length Dach put an end to the procedural controversy. Early next morning, he announced, before the start of the final readings, he would confront the regimental secretary. Then he bade us all, in God's name, to retire for the night.

17

Greflinger—to relieve the suspense—had gone fishing. From the weir of the fulling mill he had cast a net into the outer Ems and set out lines; but the two other youngsters found deep, blessed, scarcely dream-ruffled sleep. The repeated exertions of the night before, when, stirred by the full moon, they and Greflinger had lain with the maids, had made them heavy-headed enough to fall straight from the general gloom into the attic straw. Scheffler was breathing regularly before Birken; whereas the three maids found no rest when the last cooking fire had burned down but, along with the town wenches, fell to those musketeers not on guard duty. The night life in the stable could be heard across the courtyard and through the front windows of the tavern. Perhaps to counter the din with sounds of equal volume, the publishers and authors kept themselves awake with literary arguments in several of the rooms.

Paul Gerhardt found sleep by praying, long in vain but then successfully, for deliverance from the far-echoing lusts of the flesh. Dach and Albert—they, too, experienced in dealing with sinful noise—guided their fatigue to its goal. In their room, where nothing of Schütz remained, they read the Bible to each other— the Book of Job, needless to say. . . .

But restlessness remained. A searching for everything and nothing. Perhaps it was still the influence of the full moon that brought movement into the house and kept us restless. Hardly less fat, it hung over the Emshagen. I'd have liked to bark at it, to howl with the tavern dogs. But with the poets I carried controversy, thesis and antithesis, along corridors and up and down stairs. After years of practice, Rist and Zesen were at it again—two purifiers of the language, wrangling over spelling, accent, the naturalization of foreign words, neologisms. Theological entanglements soon developed. For they were all religious. Every form of Protestant opinionatedness was put forward. Every man among them thought himself nearer to God. None permitted doubt to test the fabric of his faith. Only Logau, in whom a freethinker lurked (unavowed), infuriated Lutherans and Calvinists alike with his obnoxious irony. All you had to do, he cried out, was listen a while to the Old German and New Evangelical scholasticism, and you'd be tempted to turn Papist then and there. A good thing that Paul Gerhardt was already asleep. And better still that old Weckherlin reminded the gentlemen of their deferred project, the German poets' appeal for peace.

The final script, cried the publishers, must deplore the economic situation of the printing houses. And of the writers, Schneuber demanded. They should at last be enabled to write poems celebrating the marriages, baptisms, and funerals of common citizens, not just those of the upper classes. True peace, said Moscherosch, required such justice for every Christian man and woman. He even wanted the manifesto to include a price scale for commissioned poems, graduated according to class and fortune. So that not only the noble and patrician burgher should be dispatched on his last journey with rhymes, but the poor man as well.

And so Moscherosch, Rist, and Harsdörffer sat down at a table in Hofmannswaldau and Gryphius's room, while the others, after leaving elaborate instructions, went to bed. Hesitantly, peace crept into a house full of restless guests. Not far from the four drafters, Gryphius slept stormily, as though wrestling with the angel; actually he should have been numbered among the authors of the manifesto, for his head, even in sleep teeming with words, cast its shadow on the manuscript.

When the drafters decided they were satisfied, not, to be sure, with the newly framed text but with the effort they had contributed, and each for himself (with a head full of several-times-rejected sentences) collapsed into bed, only Harsdörffer remained sleepless, tormented, as he lay across from the deeply breathing Endter, and not only by the moon in the window. Time and again he made a decision and rejected it. He wanted to count sheep but instead counted the gold buttons on Gelnhausen's doublet. He wanted to get up, but stayed in bed. He longed to go out, along corridors, down steps, and across the courtyard, and hadn't the strength to throw off his eiderdown. One force tugged at him, another held him still. He wanted to go out to Gelnhausen, but couldn't have said exactly what he wanted of Gelnhausen. At one moment it was anger, at another it was a brotherly feeling toward Stoffel that tried to pull him out of bed and across the courtyard. In the end Harsdörffer took to hoping that Gelnhausen would come to him, so they might weep together—about their wretched lot, about the wheel of fortune, about the delusion beneath the glitter, about the wretchedness of the world. . . .

But Gelnhausen was shedding his tears with landlady Libuschka. She, an old woman, to him forever young, his bottomless barrel and bucket to pour himself out into, his wet nurse, his bed of sloth, his leech, held him close and listened her fill. Once again everything had gone wrong. Nothing he attempted turned out right. Again he had blundered. Yet he had only wanted to do a bit of trading in Coesfeld, where his acquaintance with the nuns of the Marienbrink convent extended under their habits, and not to forage as was customary in those parts. One of the eleven devils must have driven the Swedes within range of their muskets. He was good and sick of soldiering. He was going to cut his ties with Mars once and for all and content himself from then on with small, peaceful gains. Maybe as an innkeeper. Just as she, the restless Courage, had settled down as landlady Libuschka. He already knew of a good place for sale. Near Offenburg. The Silver Star, it was called. If Courage could do it, so could he. All it took was gumption. And only a little while ago, the great Schütz, who had every reason to be hard on him, had advised him—good, fatherly advice—to settle down. When he, Stoffel, had wanted to go down on his knees to Schütz and beg forgiveness, the world-famous man had spoken kindly, told him about his childhood in Weissenfels on the Saale, and how ably his father had managed his spacious inn, At the Sign of the Archer.* And how under the great bay window there had been a stone statue of an ass playing the bagpipes. Stoffel, Schütz had said laughing, had just such an ass inside him, and he proceeded to call him Simplex. Whereupon he had asked the worthy gentleman whether he thought Simplex and the bagpipe-playing ass

*German *Schütze* = "archer" or "marksman."—TRANS.

capable of operating a spacious inn. Of that and far more, had been the kindly gentleman's reply.

But since landlady Libuschka from Bragoditz in Bohemia, whom Stoffel never wearied of calling (sometimes affectionately, sometimes disparagingly) Courage, had no confidence in his ability to run an inn, and only scoffed at him—with his "far more," she suggested, Maestro Sagittario must have been referring to the volume of his debts and accruing interest—and went on to deliver herself of the opinion that, apart from the ability to sit still, what he lacked to become a successful innkeeper was the subtle art of distinguishing between good customers and those who evaporated without paying, Gelnhausen, who had thus far listened in silence, went livid with rage. Old sow! Gallowsbird! Whore! Cesspit! he cried. He called her a witch, whose entire fortune had been made by whoring. Ever since she had fallen in with Mansfeld's cavalry in the Bohemian Forest, Courage had laid herself open to all comers. Whole regiments had ridden through. You had only to scratch her French face paint to see the whore underneath. She, the barren thistle, who could never bear a child, had tried to palm a brat off on him. But one thing was sure! He'd get even. Word for word. As soon as he got clear of the army and his future inn began to prosper, he would cut himself the finest pens. Yes indeed! And in his finely spun, crudely wrought manuscript he would depict the life that had come his way.

And, along with the fun and the horror, the venal splendor of Courage's body. He'd known her checkered history ever since the whisperings at the spa: the rake-offs she had taken, the ill-gotten gains she had stashed away. And what Courage had then kept secret from him, his crony Harum-Scarum had told him down to the smallest detail: how she had plied her trade in the camp outside Mantua, what magic she had kept in little bottles, how many Brunswickers had passed over her . . . everything! He would put the whoring and thieving of close to thirty years on paper—in accordance with all the rules of art—and make them live forever.

That handed landlady Libuschka a laugh. The mere idea made her shake. Her laughter drove first Gelnhausen, then herself out of bed. Did he, Stoffel, the simple-minded regimental secretary, think he could compete with the art of the learned gentlemen now gathered in her house? Did he, whose mouth overflowed with foolishness, hope to keep pace with Master Gryphius's verbal cascade, with the eloquent wisdom of Johann Rist? No, really, did he think he could rival the daring, lavishly ornamented wit of Masters Harsdörffer and Moscherosch? Had he, whom no magister had taught how to put a sentence together or count feet, the gall to measure his metric skill with that of the acute Master Logau? Did he, who didn't even know what religion he believed in, suppose he could drown out Master Gerhardt's pious hymns? Did he, who had started life as a wagoner and stableboy, then turned common soldier, and only lately risen to the rank of regimental secretary, he who had never learned anything but murder, robbing corpses, highway robbery, and perhaps in a pinch the art of keeping regimental records, aspire to make his way with hymns and sonnets, with witty and entertaining satires, odes, and elegies? Why, while he was about it, wouldn't he pen deep-thinking treatises for the instruction of others? Did he, Stoffel, really imagine that he could become a poet?

The landlady didn't laugh long. Opposition caught up with her in mid-sentence. She was still scoffing—how she would just love to see the flyspecks this Stoffel would put on paper about her, Libuschka, of noble Bohemian family! —when Gelnhausen struck. With his fist. It hit her left eye. She fell, pulled herself to her feet, staggered around the cluttered storeroom that served as her bedchamber, tumbled over saddles and boots, groped, and found a wooden pestle of the kind used for pounding dried peas. With one eye, for the blow had shut the other, she looked for the maggot-shitter, the peeping Tom, the redbeard, the pockmarked devil, but all she could find was junk. She struck pitifully at thin air.

Gelnhausen was already outside. Across the moon-bright courtyard and through alder bushes, he ran to the outer Ems, where, weeping, he met the weeping Harsdörffer, who, sleepless with misery, hadn't been able to stay in bed for long. Off to one side, on the weir of the fulling mill, Greflinger might have been seen fishing. But Harsdörffer saw nothing, and beside him Gelnhausen was also sightless.

The two of them sat on the steep embankment until morning. They didn't say much to each other. Even their unhappiness had no need of being exchanged. Not a word of reproof or repentance. How beautifully the river embedded itself in their vale of tears. A nightingale gave answer to their gloom. Perhaps the experienced Harsdörffer told Stoffel how to make a name for oneself as a poet. Perhaps Stoffel was eager even then to know if he should try to emulate the Spanish storytellers. Perhaps that night on the bank of the Ems supplied the poet with that first line—"Come, balm of night, O nightingale"—which was later to open the song of the Spessart Mountain hermit. Perhaps Harsdörffer already warned his young colleague against pirated editions and publishers' greed. And perhaps the two friends ended by sleeping side by side.

Not until voices and slamming doors from the Bridge Tavern announced the coming of day were they jolted awake. Where the Ems divided before separating Emshagen Island from the town wall on one side and from Tecklenburg territory on the other, crested grebes were rocking in the water. Looking toward the fulling mill, I saw that Greflinger had pulled in his net and lines.

Speaking into the sun behind the birches on the opposite shore, Harsdörffer said the congress might pronounce a sentence. Gelnhausen said: I've been there before.

18

Much used as were the three maids who served it, pathetically swollen (as though one-eyed) as was landlady Libuschka's face as she looked on, the morning soup did not lack strength. And no one would have dreamed of complaining, for the tasty brew had obviously been boiled down from the goose giblets, the pigs' kidneys, and the (crowned, then uncrowned) sheep's head left over from the night before. In their weakened state, as the gentlemen came creeping from their rooms, their need for piping-hot sustenance was greater than their by no means negligible spiritual hangover, which, however, did not express itself until they all, from Albert and Dach to Weckherlin and Zesen, had spooned up their soup.

First—while Birken and others were still bending over their seconds—new trouble was aired. Weckherlin had been robbed. A leather purse full of silver shillings had vanished from his room. Though the old man dismissed Lauremberg's prompt assumption that it must have been Greflinger, the suspicion that the vagabond had snatched the purse was reinforced by Schneuber's report that he had seen him playing dice with the musketeers. And a further mark against Greflinger was the fact—which no one could overlook—that he was still absent. He was lying in the bushes on the riverbank, beside dead or still-quivering fishes, sleeping off the weariness of his night's exertions.

After Dach, visibly worn by the accumulated unpleasantness, had promised that the theft would soon be cleared up and gone so far as to vouch for Greflinger, the wretchedness of the previous day repeated on them: What were they to do with this horror? Could they go on reading from manuscripts as if nothing had happened? Wouldn't all poetry sound flat after that butcher's feast? Were the assembled poets still entitled, after such dreadful revelations—possibly a thief in their midst!—to look upon themselves as honorable men, let alone to issue a morally motivated appeal for peace?

Birken asked: had they not, in gobbling up that bandit's food, entangled themselves in complicity? No satire, Lauremberg complained, could accommodate so much bestiality. As though the sacramental wine were still at work within him, Gryphius's imposing frame disgorged bundles of words. And Weckherlin declared that such a feast would make even gluttonous London, that veritable Moloch, vomit. Whereupon Zesen, Rist, and Gerhardt outdid themselves in images of guilt, repentance, and atonement.

(What was not expressed were the private troubles underlying this cosmic nausea: Gerhardt's worry, for example, that he might never be gratified with a parsonage; Moscherosch's bitter fear that his friends might stop believing in his Moorish descent and, on the mere strength of his name, start calling him a Jew to his face, stoning him with words; or Weckherlin's grief over the recent death of his wife, which stayed with him through all his jests. And the old man also dreaded his return to London, the loneliness in Gardiner's Lane, where he had been living for years but remained a foreigner. Soon he would be pensioned, his place taken by Milton, another poet but a partisan of Cromwell. And other fears . . .)

And yet, for all his tribulations, Simon Dach seemed to have gathered strength overnight. Pulling himself up to stalwart middle height, he observed that each and every one of them had a lifetime ahead in which to dwell on his recent increment of sin. They had all enjoyed their morning soup, and there was no need of further lamentations. Since he did not see Gelnhausen at table and since it was hardly to be expected that his contrition would allow him to attend additional readings, there seemed to be no point in trying him, especially since such a trial would seem presumptuous and pharisaical. Feeling sure that friend Rist, not only as a poet but still more as a clergyman, agreed with him, and gleaning from Gerhardt's silence that even so pious and rigorous a Christian was of the same mind, he would now—if Lauremberg would finally stop chattering with the maids—announce the program for the day and once again commend the meeting—what remained of it—to God's inexhaustible goodness.

After taking his Albert aside and bidding him look for the still regrettably absent Greflinger, Dach read the names of those who had yet to read: Czepko, Hofmannswaldau, Weckherlin, Schneuber. When calls rang out begging him finally, for the delectation of all, to read his lament for the lost cucumber bower, Dach tried to get out of it by invoking the shortage of time. But when Schneuber (at the suggestion of Moscherosch) undertook to forgo his contribution, it was agreed that Dach would conclude the session with a reading of his poem; for Dach wished to devote a special session, apart from the poetry reading, to the final drafting of the appeal for peace, demanded by Rist and others, in the form of a political manifesto—two new versions had meanwhile been submitted. "Therefore," he said, "we will not let the discussion of war and peace obtrude into our Muses' grove, the cultivation of which must be ever on our minds. For, undeterred by fences, a frost might nip our shady cucumber vine, causing it to wither, as, so the Scriptures tell us, befell Jonah."

His concern was shared. It was decided that the appeal for peace would be discussed in detail and completed between the last reading and the simple (as unanimously demanded) noonday meal. After the meal—the landlady promised to make it "honest," that is, meager—the assembled poets would disperse, each in his own direction.

At length order was put into chaos. Thanks to Simon Dach's protective interpretation of his name,* we were all of good heart and witty in groups. Some of us were even growing frolicsome—young Birken wanted to crown Dach with a garland—when Lauremberg's shouted question—against what bedpost had the landlady blackened her eye?—revived the misery of the day before.

After holding it in for much too long, Libuschka spoke out: it wasn't the work of a bedpost but of Gelnhausen's manly vigor. Apparently, she said, it hadn't yet dawned on the gentlemen what a foul trick that peasant lout had played on them. Everything that crossed the fellow's lips was a tissue of lies and fabulation, and that included his confession to Sagittario. Gelnhausen's horsemen and musketeers had not commandeered those provisions from any Swedes, no, they themselves had taken them, professional raiders, that's what they were, that smooth-talking bandit had lived up to his reputation. His green doublet was feared from Soest

*Dach = roof.—TRANS.

to Vechta. Any virgin pleading with him for mercy would be wasting her breath. His methods could make the mute talk. And incidentally, the church silver, altar cloths, and sacramental wine had been hornswoggled out of the whores' convent in Coesfeld. The Hessian guard was no help, a weasel like Gelnhausen could always get through. No loyalty to either camp. He swore only by his own flag. And if Master Harsdörffer still believed that the papal nuncio himself had given Stoffel the little volume of the playful *Conversation Pieces for Women* to have it dedicated by the author, she would have to cut the cords of his vanity: Gelnhausen had bribed one of the nuncio's servants to steal it from the cardinal's library. The pages hadn't even been cut. That was how finely Gelnhausen spun his web of lies. For years the fellow had been hoodwinking the finest gentlemen no less effectively. No devil could hold a candle to him. She knew it to her sorrow.

With difficulty Dach succeeded in relieving the general consternation and his own—a little. Harsdörffer drooped. Anger darkened the usually even-tempered Czepko. If Logau had not remarked appeasingly that birds of a feather flock together, another long argument could have been feared. Gratefully Dach clapped his hands. Enough now! He would look into these accusations. One lie had a way of leading to another. He hoped they would all close their ears to this new hubbub. From then on the poets

161

should concentrate on their own calling; if not, their art would fail them.

Consequently Dach's first impulse was one of anger when his Albert suddenly led Greflinger into the taproom. He was already beginning to shower the long-haired young fellow with reproaches—what had got into him? Where had he been? Had he made off with Weckherlin's purse?—when, like all the others, he saw what Greflinger had brought back in two buckets: barbels, roaches, and other fish. Draped in the net and hung with fishing lines—which he had borrowed the day before from the widow of the Telgte town fisherman—the young man stood there like a portrait. He had fished all night. Not even the Danube could boast better barbels. Fried crisp, even the bony roach would prove tasty. The whole lot could be served up for their noonday meal. And if anyone called him a thief, he'd tell him what for.

No one was inclined to challenge Greflinger's fists. All looked forward to the honest fish. Behind Dach, the company moved into the great hall, where their symbol, the thistle, stood beside the unoccupied footstool.

19

No one hesitated. All, including even Gerhardt, stood up for their literary undertaking, prepared to fight for it. The war had taught them to live with adversity. Dach was not alone; no one was willing to be put off. Not Zesen or Rist, much as those two purists and purifiers of the language might quarrel between themselves; neither the commoners nor the nobles, still less since under Dach's chairmanship the classes had spontaneously shaken off their structure. No one wanted the meeting to break up—not the unknown Scheffler, not the vagrant, always suspect Greflinger, not even Schneuber, who, on instructions from the uninvited Magister Rompler, kept looking for ways of fomenting trouble; and definitely not the older men, Buchner and Weckherlin, who had never been deeply interested in anything but poetry; even Gryphius, easy as he found it to repudiate all work in progress as vain delusion, stood firm. No one was willing to give up merely because reality had once again put in an objection and cast mud at art.

Accordingly, all those who had gathered in the semicircle remained seated on their chairs, stools, and barrels when Gelnhausen—the instant Czepko had taken his place between the thistle and Simon Dach and prepared to read— climbed from the garden into the great hall through an open window. With his red beard he sat down on the window seat and had nothing but summer behind him. Since the company showed no sign of restlessness, since a paralysis born of determination held them still, Dach felt justified in giving Czepko the sign. Having poems to read, the Silesian took a deep breath.

But then—before he could utter so much as a line—Gelnhausen spoke in a voice that purported to be modest but carried an overtone of mockery. He was glad, he said, that in spite of the trickery that Master Schütz had so sternly censured, but then like a true Christian forgiven, the illustrious and widely famed gentlemen who were forgathered under Apollo's aegis, now and for all time, had readmitted him, the peasant lout escaped from the Spessart Mountains, to the end that he, the simple-minded Stoffel, might continue his education until such time as he, too, might learn to create order out of everything he had read, which lay helter-skelter in his mind. Thus instructed, he hoped to climb into art as he had just climbed through the window and—should the Muses be propitious—become a poet.

Only then did pent-up rage explode. If he had sat still—all right. If by quietly sitting there he had helped them to show magnanimity—better yet. But the pretension to be their equal was too much for the far-traveled members of the Fruit-bearing, Upright, Pegnitz, and German-minded societies. They unburdened themselves with cries of "Murdering scoundrel! Liar!" Rist shouted, "Popish agent!" Someone (Gerhardt?) went so far as to cry out, "Get thee hence, Satan!"

They jumped up, shook their fists, and would probably, Lauremberg in the lead, have dealt blows, if Dach had not grasped the situation and reacted to a sign from Harsdörffer. With his voice, which even in earnest took an easy, casual tone and always seemed to say, "It's all right; don't take yourselves so seriously," he pacified the company and then asked The Playful One to explain himself.

Addressing Gelnhausen as a friend, Harsdörffer asked him rather gently whether he confessed to the crimes that landlady Libuschka had added to his account. He listed all her accusations, concluding with what was most galling to him personally, the lie about the copy of his *Conversation Pieces for Women* stolen from the nuncio's library.

Now predominantly self-assured, Gelnhausen replied that he no longer had any wish to defend himself. Yes and by all means yes. He and his horsemen and musketeers had acted in the spirit of the times, just as the gentlemen here assembled were constrained to act in the spirit of the times when they wrote poems in praise of princes to whom murder and arson came as naturally as their daily prayers, whose robberies, out of all proportion to the bit of food he had made off with, were blessed by the priests, who switched loyalties as easily as they changed their shirts, and whose repentance lasted no longer than a paternoster. He, on the other hand, the accused Stoffel, had long repented and would long continue to repent of having helped so unworldly a company to find lodgings, of having protected them from bandits with his horsemen and musketeers, and, to top it all, of having sullied himself by supplying them with three kinds of roast meat, delectable wine, white bread, and spicy condiments. All that, as was now evident, without advantage to himself and purely out of gratitude for certain lessons received. Yes, it was true, he had wished to give the learned poets pleasure with his fantasy about the massed greetings from the princely, royal, and imperial ambassadors assembled at the Münster chapter house. Similarly, he had wished to please Harsdörffer, who had thus far been so well disposed to him and whom he loved like his own Heartsbrother,* with a mild deception; wherein he had been

*A character in Grimmelshausen's novel *Simplicissimus.*—ED.

successful, for the Nuremberger had taken unfeigned delight in the papal nuncio's request for a dedication. What did it really matter whether Chigi actually wanted the dedication, whether he could or should have wanted it, or whether the whole story was no more than a pleasant fantasy sprung from the brain of the here accused Stoffel? If because they were without power the gentlemen were also without standing in their country—and that was the truth!—a credible show must be made of their nonexistent standing. Since when were poets so intent on dry, flat truth? What made their left hands so dull when their right hands were so practiced in exalting their rhymed truths to the realm of the incredible? Must poetic lies be printed and published before they could be ranked as truth? Or, in other terms, was the bargaining in land and people now entering its fourth year in Münster more authentic, not to say more honorable, than the commerce with accented and unaccented syllables, with words and spoken sounds and images, being conducted here at Telgte's Ems Gate?

At first the company had listened to Gelnhausen with reserve, then here and there with repressed laughter, thoughtful headshaking, cool attentiveness, or like Hofmannswaldau, with visible relish—but the dominant reaction was one of amazement. Dach gave frequent signs of amusement at the consternation gathered around him. There was challenge in the look that he trained on the silent circle: was no one going to refute the man's insolent wit?

After stopping to quote Herodotus and Plautus in Latin, Buchner concluded with a quotation from Stoffel himself: That is the truth! Whereupon Logau suggested that they let the matter rest. At last, he said, they knew who they were; only jesters could hold up such accurate mirrors.

That didn't satisfy Greflinger. No, he cried, it was not a jester, but the common people, who were not present at this meeting, who had told him the truth. Stoffel was his, Greflinger's, kinsman. He, too, the vagrant peasant boy, had been tossed about by life before he had a chance to sniff at books. If anyone spoke of throwing Stoffel out, he, too, would go.

At length Harsdörffer declared that after thus being made a fool of he knew what to write about vanity. Brother Gelnhausen should kindly stay and regale them with further unpalatable truths.

But already Stoffel was standing in the window opening, ready to take his leave. No. Mars was putting him back in harness. The Münster chapter house had entrusted him with a message to take to Cologne and beyond: The chapter would have to pay nine hundred thousand talers in indemnities if the Hessians were to evacuate Coesfeld, the Swedes Vechta, and the Dutch Bevergern. This war gave promise of costing money for a long time to come. He, however, would depart with a promise that cost nothing, the promise that they would hear from him again. True, years and years might pass before he had refurbished his knowledge, bathed in Harsdörffer's sources, studied Moscherosch's craft, gleaned rules from this and that treatise, but then he would be present: as lively as you please, though tucked away in countless printed pages. But let no one expect mincing pastorals, conventional obituaries, complicated figure poems, sensitive soul-blubber, or well-behaved rhymes for church congregations. No, he would let every foul smell out of the bag; a chronicler, he would bring back the long war as a word-butchery, let loose gruesome laughter, and give the language license to be what it is: crude and soft-spoken, whole and stricken, here French-ified, there melancholicky, but always drawn from the casks of life. Yes, he would write! By Jupiter, Mercury, and Apollo, he would!

With that Gelnhausen removed himself from the window. But, both feet in the garden, he turned back with an ultimate home truth. From his breeches pocket he drew a purse and tossed it up twice in his hand, so making its silvery contents known. He laughed briefly and, before throwing the purse through the window to land just short of the thistle, said that it still remained for him to deposit this small thing he had found. For one of the gentlemen had left his purse in Courage's bed. Enjoyable as it was to visit the landlady of the Bridge Tavern, no one should be overcharged for his brief pleasure.

Only then was he really and truly gone. Gelnhausen left the assembled poets alone among themselves. Already we missed him. From outside there was no other sound than the hoarse braying of the mules. Well rounded, the leather purse lay beside the thistle. Old Weckherlin arose, took a few steps with dignity, picked up the purse, and returned calmly to his chair. No one laughed. Gelnhausen's speech still held power, which no one wanted to break. Finally Dach said without transition: Now that everything had been found and cleared up, there was to be zealous reading. Otherwise the morning would escape them with Stoffel.

20

I, too, was sorry to see Christoffel Gelnhausen, once more in his green doublet and feathered hat, leave with his imperial horsemen and musketeers. Not a single gold button was missing from his doublet. In spite of all that had happened, he had suffered no harm.

That was one more reason why no word of reconciliation could fall between him and landlady Libuschka. Unmoved, she looked on from the tavern door as his little company saddled horses, harnessed one of the covered wagons requisitioned in Oesede, and (taking the child-size bronze Apollo with them) left the Bridge Tavern—Gelnhausen in the lead.

Since I now know more than Libuschka, gray with hatred, could have suspected in the tavern doorway, I will speak for Stoffel. His *Courasche*—

published in Nuremberg under the pen name Philarchus Grossus von Trommenheim roughly a quarter century after his silent parting from the landlady of the Bridge Tavern, under the long title *Defiance to Simplex or Detailed and Most Strange Description of the Arch-Trickster, Trollop, and Most Notorious Rogue Courage,* and distributed by Felssecker, his publisher— was the late fulfillment of his vows of vengeance. Since the author of *Simplicissimus,* which had appeared two years before, lets his Courage speak with her own voice and settle accounts with herself, his book is a paper monument to a sturdy and unstable, childless yet inventive, vulnerable and embattled woman, man-mad in skirts, manly in breeches, making the most of her beauty, a woman both pitiful and lovable, all the more so since the author of all subsequent "Simpliciads," who occasionally called himself Hans Christoffel von Grimmelshausen, granted his "Courage" paper on which to mete out powerful blows to Simplex, his very own self; for what stirred Gelnhausen and Libuschka together like milk and vinegar was an excess of love, or call it hate.

Not until the regimental secretary and his men were crossing the outer Ems bridge on their way to Warendorf (and thence to Cologne) and out of the landlady's sight did her right hand attempt a motion that might have been taken for waving good-bye. I, too, would have liked to wave good-bye to Stoffel, but thought it more important to attend the last readings of the assembled poets in the great hall, where the thistle stood significantly. Having been there from the very beginning, I also wanted to witness the end. For fear of missing something.

There were no further interruptions. Daniel von Czepko, a Silesian jurist and counselor to the dukes of Brieg, in whom, since his period of study in Strassburg, the God-and-man-fusing mysticism fired by the shoemaker Böhme had flickered beneath a show of indifference, that reserved, little-noticed man whose friend I should have liked to be, read several epigrams, the form of which (alexandrine couplets) was also congenial to Gryphius and Logau. Young Scheffler had attempted something similar, though his efforts were still crude, the antitheses not yet carried to their ultimate clarity. Possibly because in the ensuing discussion period the Breslau medical student seemed (though startled) to understand Czepko's "beginning in the end, end in the beginning," and because on the day before Czepko had been the only one (apart from Schütz) to grasp the overall meaning of the student's confused offering, they conceived a friendship that remained possible even after Scheffler became the Catholic Angelus Silesius and published his *Cherubinic Wanderer,* whereas Czepko's chief work, his collected epigrams, found no publisher—unless perhaps the author held them back.

In keeping with their subsequent lack of success, Czepko's couplets caught the attention of few of the assembled poets. Who had ears for so much silence? Only one poem, a political piece that Czepko referred to as a fragment—"The fatherland is where freedom and justice are. It knows us not and we know not that distant star"—met with wider approval. After Moscherosch and Rist it was again the diminutive Magister Buchner who threw out his chest and interpreted Czepko's lines into a chaotic world hungering for harmony, in the process quoting Augustine, Erasmus, and time and time again himself. In the end, the magister's speech aroused more applause than Czepko's marginally praised poem. (Buchner was still extemporizing after the author had relinquished the stool beside the thistle.)

Next the seat up front was taken by a gaunt, long-limbed man who didn't know what to do with his legs. The surprise was general when Hofmann von Hofmannswaldau, who had failed thus far to distinguish himself with any published work and was regarded as a mere literary dilettante, expressed his readiness to read. Even Gryphius, who had known the wealthy nobleman since their student days together in Danzig and Leiden—he had encouraged the rather passive aesthete to write—seemed surprised and even a bit appalled when Hofmannswaldau insisted on reading.

Cleverly exaggerating his embarrassment, Hofmannswaldau apologized for his presumption in wishing to sit between Dach and the thistle, but owned that he was itching to submit his efforts to criticism. He then astonished the company with a genre deriving from Ovid, new to Germany, and cultivated only in foreign parts, for his selection consisted of so-called "heroes' letters," which he introduced with a tale, "The Life and Love of Peter Abelard and Helisse."

This is the story of an ambitious young scholar in Paris who is occasionally driven by academic intrigues to take refuge in the provinces. Back in Paris, he outshines even the famous theologian Anselme, and becomes a universal favorite. Finally a certain Folbert employs him to give his niece private instruction, but instead of confining himself to Latin, Abelard falls madly in love with his pupil, who falls madly in love with her teacher. "In short, their scholarship suffers from a different sort of assiduity. . . ." But their lessons continue and the consequence is a "learned wantoning," which takes root. The teacher removes his pregnant pupil to the home of his sister in Brittany, and there she is delivered of a boy. Although the young mother has no desire to marry and protests vehemently "that it would please her more to be called his mistress than his wedded wife," the teacher insists on a simple marriage ceremony, which is performed in Paris, while the child stays in Brittany with Abelard's sister. But since Uncle Folbert is hostile to the marriage, Abelard hides his pupil and wife in a convent near Paris; whereupon Folbert, infuriated by his niece's flight, bribes Abelard's servant "to unlock his master's bedchamber at night and castrate him with the help of some likewise bribed ruffians," which is irrevocably done.

The loss of Abelard's wantoning equipment is the subject of the two ensuing letters written in alternately rhymed alexandrines and periphrasing unspeakable horror in a courtly refinement of the Opitzian manner: "I thought the fire of passion was no such grievous thing; No bramblebush, thought I, will bar my chosen way; On thinnest ice I thought to go a-wantoning. But now, alas, I find a knife hath spoiled my play. . . ."

Since form was everything to Hofmannswaldau, he had asked leave before starting to read to call Abelard's pupil "Helisse" for the sake of the rhyme: Helisse now tries, in her letter to Abelard, to overbalance the loss of his equipment with higher love: "And though your sweetsome lips moved me too carnally, Built a lubricious house with roses all entwined, My passion never stripped my intellect from me, And every kiss I gave was leveled at your mind. . . ."

Little as the assembled poets found to criticize in Hofmannswaldau's art—Buchner declared that it far outdid Opitz and even Fleming!—the morality of the story stuck bittersweet in several of their craws. The first to speak was Rist with his eternal: Where does it lead? What good can come of it? Then indignation poured from Gerhardt, who had heard nothing but gilded sin in all that "vain feast of words." When, after Lauremberg's grumbling about "artificial rhymes," young Birken took umbrage at those horrible goings-on, Greflinger asked him if he had forgotten what instrument he had recently used on the maids in the straw. No, Birken replied, he had no objection to the implement either before or after the cutting, what he minded was the smooth and slippery manner. A pity that Gelnhausen was gone. He would have shown the bloody butchery and Helisse's forced continence naked and screaming.

When many (but not Gryphius) then asked leave to speak, wishing to carp at Abelard's genitals, Simon Dach said he had heard enough about the ill-reputed but useful implement. The tale, he owned, had moved him. But, he went on, let no one forget the touching end, which at long last unites the lovers in one grave, where their bones are at pains to intertwine. On hearing that, he said, the tears had come to his eyes.

As though all this criticism had been known to him in advance, Hofmannswaldau took the flood of words with a smile. Originally suggested by Dach, it had since become the rule that the reader should not speak in his own defense. For this same reason Weckherlin submitted unresisting to the excess cleverness that filled the air after the reading of his ode entitled "A Kiss."

The old man had written this poem—and all his other literary work, for that matter—when still young, almost thirty years before. Then, because there was nothing to hold him in Stuttgart, he had become an agent in the service of the Elector Palatine and finally, hoping to make himself more useful to the Palatinate, gone to work for the English government. Since then he had written nothing worth mentioning, only hundreds of subversive secret-agent's letters to Opitz, Niclassius, Oxenstierna, and others. . . . And yet Weckherlin's playful, sometimes amateurish little poems, written years before the appearance of Opitz's book on German poetics, had retained their freshness, all the more so because, thanks to his Swabian tongue, the old man managed to use his delivery to help his frivolous verses and sometimes dreary rhymes— "honeyed lips"/"soul's eclipse"—over the rough spots.

Weckherlin had let it be known at the outset that, since his duties as traveling undersecretary of state left him sufficient leisure, he was planning to rework (handling the rise and fall, the accented and unaccented syllables, more proficiently) the rhymed sins of his youth, most of which had been modeled on French originals and dated from the old prewar days, and have them reprinted. He knew, he said, that the young men thought him a fossil. In his opinion only the late lamented Bober Swan and the worthy Augustus Buchner had published anything helpful about German prosody, and that was since his time.

In the discussion period he was applauded. Because he was still around. We younger men had thought the old fellow dead. We were surprised to see the precursor of our young art alive and kicking; he had even climbed into Libuschka's bed like a man still capable of light-footed odes.

Though Rist abominated all bawdy verse, he nevertheless, though an Opitzian, came out in favor of Weckherlin. Buchner, plunging deep into the past, made common cause with Zesen and Gerhardt, who had been his students in Wittenberg, in sending the rest of the company back to versification school. Logau was as silent as before.

Then Simon Dach had to change chairs and asked old Weckherlin to guard the armchair in which he seemed to have taken root. Dach's long "Lament on the Ultimate Decline and Fall of the Musical Cucumber Bower and Garden" is an attempt at an epicedium to console his friend Albert for the loss of his garden, destroyed by mud and roadbuilder's rubble on Lomse Island in the river Pregel. In spacious alexandrines it relates the laying out of the garden, in which Albert was assisted by his tippling and now spade-wielding organ-blower, the friends' literary and musical entertainments and idyllic pleasures—their happily discovered harmony. Far away the war is sowing hunger plague desolation; closer at hand burghers are wrangling, preachers quarreling. Just as Jonah under his biblical gourd threatened sinful Nineveh with God's wrath, so Dach admonishes his tripartite Königsberg. His lament over the destruction of Magdeburg (where he had studied as a young man) leads to generalized lamentation

179

over Germany's self-dismemberment. A condemnation of war—"So prompt are men to draw the sword of war and death, So pitifully slow to return it to its sheath"—is followed by the yearning for a just peace: "Oh, if the pain and loss of others made us wise, We surely then would find grace in our Maker's eyes." But, adjuring himself and his Albert to do what they can and make the best of the times—"To counter their duress however hard they press"—Dach concludes with the lofty demands of poetry, which will outlive their cucumber bower: "Provided life and spirit inspire our poetry, Each line will give us part in immortality."

That appealed to us. Spoken from the hearts of all there assembled. Though at present they had no power and little glory, since the present was dominated by war and land grabbing, religious oppression and short-term greed, they aspired with the help of poetry to gain future power and secure eternal glory. This slight, rather ridiculous power helped them to well-paid commissions. Wealthy burghers and a sprinkling of princes, suspecting themselves to be more mortal than poets, hoped that verses, for the most part hastily written, commemorating their marriages, deaths, and illustrious deeds, would carry them into eternity, name and all.

Even more than any of the others, Simon Dach earned supplementals with commissioned poems. Whenever fees were compared at meetings with his colleagues, he had his bitter joke ready: "At Marriages and Deaths, they hire me as their mummer, Just as they might engage a baker or a plumber." Dach even owed his Kneiphof professorship to certain encomiums that he had tossed off in the late thirties, when the elector made his entrance into the city.

Consequently, after the company had richly complimented the lament for the cucumber bower, Gryphius's ambiguous demur—"You pen three hundred verses before my three I write, A laurel tree grows slowly, a cucumber overnight"—was taken as a malicious allusion to Dach's forced prolixity. When, soon thereafter, Rist first praised the moral content of the lament, but then took umbrage at the mythological allusions—the comparison, for example, of gutted Magdeburg with Thebes, Corinth, Carthage—and at the invocation of the Muse Melpomene, Buchner was prepared for rebuttal even before Zesen. No foreign influence, he declared, desecrated this poem. The whole of it flowed from a German mouth. Needed for contrast, the few witnesses from antiquity were an integral part of the magnificent edifice, which was beyond compare.

From Dach's armchair old Weckherlin said: A finer conclusion could not have been found. And Harsdörffer cried out: Oh, if only we had a cucumber bower big enough for us all, to shelter us from these evil times!

There was no need to say more. Gryphius's insult had been buried beneath sufficient praise. Laughing (and as though relieved), Simon Dach

181

stood up from the stool beside the thistle. He embraced Weckherlin and led him back to his chair. Several times he paced back and forth from his armchair to the unoccupied stool and the thistle in the flowerpot. Then he said that was the end. He was glad the meeting had proceeded peaceably after all. For that he gave thanks to the Heavenly Father in the name of all there assembled. Amen. And yes, he wished to add, he had enjoyed the sessions in spite of certain vexations. At the noonday meal, before they dispersed in all directions, he would have a few more things to say. At the moment nothing occurred to him. But now—he could see that Rist and Moscherosch were restless—he would have to let politics in, that tiresome manifesto.

Thereupon Dach sat down again, bade the authors of the appeal for peace come forward, and, when Logau's objection provoked disorder, cautioned his charges: But no fighting, children.

21

No! he cried several times. No, before we had re-entered the great hall; no, when we all sat gathered around Dach and the thistle. And when Rist and Moscherosch finished reading the drafts of the manifesto, Logau was still shouting: No! Before and after. Absolutely: No!

He termed everything wretched. Rist's thund'rous words, the bourgeois niggling of the Strassburgers, the flowery phrases in which Hofmannswaldau stifled every conflict, Harsdörffer's Nuremberg-style maneuvering, the use of "German" or "Germany" as expletives in every half-sentence. Pitiful, hypocritical, cried Logau, who, relinquishing expressive brevity, casting off the irony that makes for succinctness, was angry enough to make a long speech aimed at stripping sentence after sentence of its verbal trumpery.

The rather frail-looking man stood in the background, distinctly apart, and spoke cuttingly over the heads of the seated gathering. Swaggering cowards, they had catered to all the parties. In one passage they wished the Swedes far away, in another they implored them to stay and help. In one sentence the Palatinate was to be restored, the next wanted to secure the favor of Bavaria through an offer of the electoral dignity. With their right hand the authors invoked the old Estate system, with their left they abjured the injustice that went with it. Only a forked tongue could in one sentence advocate freedom for every religion and in the next threaten all sects with banishment. True, the authors invoked Germany as often as a Papist invoked the Virgin Mary, but nowhere did they refer to more than a part of the whole. Loyalty industry honesty were named as German virtues, but those who were treated in truly German wise, like beasts, the peasants throughout the country, were nowhere mentioned. The authors spoke contentiously of peace, intolerantly of tolerance, and penny-pinchingly of God. And after all this talk about Germany, their praise of the fatherland stank of local interest: of Nuremberg's self-seeking, Saxony's caution, Silesian fear, Strassburgian arrogance. The whole thing was stupid and pathetic, because it hadn't been thought out.

Logau's speech inspired gloom rather than disorder. The two drafts, which differed only stylistically, passed from hand to hand, barely glanced at. Once again the poets were certain only of their impotence and their inadequate knowledge of political forces. For when (unexpectedly) old Weckherlin rose to speak, they were addressed by the one man in the entire gathering who had gained political awareness— participated in the play of forces, tasted power, shifted the weights a little, and worn himself out in the process.

The old man's tone was not at all didactic; he spoke jovially, making light of his thirty years of experience. As he talked, he strode back and forth, as though strolling from decade to decade. Sometimes he turned to Dach, sometimes he spoke out the window, as though wishing the two tethered mules to hear him, and, now rambling, now framing his thought succinctly, he pulled out the stopper. Actually the vessel was empty. Or full of rubbish. His hard work for nothing. His collected defeats. How, like the late lamented Opitz, he had been the diplomat of every conceivable party. How as a Swabian he had become an English agent and in the English service worked for the Palatinate, and how, because nothing could prosper without the Swedes, he had ended by turning double agent. And how with all his intriguing he had never achieved what had always been the aim of his slippery arts: to gain the military support of England for the Protestant cause. With all but toothless laughter Weckherlin cursed the

English Civil War and the always sprightly Palatine court, Oxenstierna's harsh coldness and the Saxon betrayal, the Germans in general, but especially and repeatedly the Swabians: their greed, their narrowness, their mania for cleanliness, and their sanctimonious prevarication. Terrifying how young the old man's hatred of everything Swabian had remained, how bitter the German quality in the Swabians and the Swabian quality in the increasing cult of Germanism rose in his gullet.

In his indictment he did not acquit himself, but called all irenicists hairsplitting fools who, to forestall the worst, had consistently prolonged the national disaster. Just as he had tried, persistently though in vain, to bring English regiments into the German war of religion, the universally honored Opitz had striven, almost to the day he died of the plague, to involve Catholic Poland in the German butchery. As though, Weckherlin cried, there had not, what with the Swedes and the French, the Spaniards and the Walloons, been butchers enough at work in the German slaughterhouse. All his and Opitz's efforts had only made matters worse!

In the end the old man had to sit down. He had run out of laughter. Drained, he could no longer participate when the others, Rist and Moscherosch in the lead, converted their hatred of everything foreign into German self-hatred. All spilled their guts. Cataclysmically they spewed their fury. Self-nourishing agitation lifted the assemblage off chairs, stools, and barrels. They beat their breasts. They wrung their hands. Where, they shouted at one another, was the so often invoked fatherland? Where had it hidden? Was there any such thing, and if so what was it like?

By the time Gerhardt, as though to console the questioners, expressed his certainty that they could count on no earthly, but only on a heavenly fatherland, Andreas Gryphius had already disengaged himself from the knot and gone looking for something. Standing beside the unoccupied stool and in front of the decomposed semicircle, he grabbed hold of the pot with the transplanted thistle and thrust the emblem and symbol of their era against the timbered ceiling. In that menacing posture he grew to mighty proportions. A giant, a savage, a groaning Moses, whose tongue was in his way until the torrent of words broke loose: barren, prickly, strewn by the wind, food for the ass, noxious weed, plague of the peasant, sent by the angry God, this thing, the thistle, was the flower and fatherland of them all! Whereupon Gryphius dropped the thistle that was Germany, dashed it to the floor in our midst.

No one could have done better. That fitted in with our mood. The fatherland had never been put before us more graphically. We seemed almost happy, glad as only Germans can be, to see our misery imaged so forcefully. Moreover, the thistle lay unharmed amid the shards and

187

scattered soil. Behold, cried Zesen, how the fatherland emerges unscathed from the severest fall!

All saw the miracle. And only then, after childlike joy over the unharmed thistle had spread, after young Birken had heaped up earth over the bared roots and Lauremberg had run for water—only after the company had thus recovered its innocence but before the usual chatter had time to start up did Simon Dach, beside whom Daniel Czepko had stationed himself, speak. During the widening, increasingly active search for the lost or no longer recognizable or totally weed-ridden fatherland, the two had been busy, here deleting, there adding, on a manuscript that, while Czepko was writing out a fair copy, Dach identified as the final version of the manifesto and read aloud.

The new text managed without any of Rist's thund'rous words. No ultimate truth was proclaimed. In plain, simple language the assembled poets entreated all parties desirous of peace not to scorn the preoccupations of the poets, who, though powerless, had acquired a claim to eternity. Without denouncing the Swedes or the French as land grabbers, without condemning the Bavarians for their haggling over territory, without so much as naming any of the warring religions, they looked into the future and pointed to some of the possible dangers and burdens implicit in the forthcoming peace: that pretexts for future wars might creep into the longed-for peace treaty; that for want of tolerance the so passionately longed-for religious peace might merely lead to further denominational strife; that the restoration of the old order, desirable as were its blessings, might—God forbid!—be accompanied by a restoration of the old, accustomed injustice; and finally, the overriding preoccupation of the assembled poets, speaking as patriots: that the empire was so threatened by dismemberment that no one could recognize in it what had once been his German fatherland.

This final version of the appeal for peace concluded with a prayer for God's blessing. As soon as the fair copy was available, it was signed without further dispute, first by Dach and Czepko, then by the others, including Logau. Whereupon the gentlemen, as though their plea had already been granted, embraced one another, some joyfully, others on the verge of tears. At last we were sure of having done something. Since the appeal lacked any grandiose gesture, Rist compensated by calling the place, day, and hour momentous.

An occasion for bell ringing. But the hand bell affixed to the door of the great hall was rung for a lesser reason. This time it was not the landlady who summoned the company to the noonday meal. Under the supervision of Greflinger, who was last to sign the manifesto, his last night's catch had been fried.

When the assembled poets poured from the

great hall into the taproom, no one paid attention to the thistle that had remained unscathed amid shards. No one was interested in anything but fish. The smell led us and we followed.

Simon Dach, who was holding the momentous manuscript, was obliged to adjust his parting words to the fish that awaited us.

22

Never has a meal been more peaceful. The fish made for gentle words around the long table. We all spoke to and about one another in soft, contented voices. And the poets listened to one another; they did not interrupt.

In the grace, which Dach assigned at the last moment to Albert, the Kneiphof cathedral organist set the tone by citing fishing-related Bible passages. After that it was easy to praise the crisp skin of the barbels and the white flesh beneath it, which fell so gently off the backbone; but then again, no one grumbled at the humbler, bony roaches. Now it could be seen how many of them—in addition to tench, perch, and one young pike—had swum into Greflinger's net or bitten at his hooks during the night. The maids brought in more and more on shallow platters, while the landlady stood with face averted at the window.

Greflinger's fish seemed to multiply miraculously. The Nurembergers, Birken in the lead, were soon obliging with pastoral rhymes. Everyone was eager to praise fish in verse, if not immediately, then at some propitious hour. And the water in the pitcher! cried Lauremberg, who along with the others—never again! Moscherosch proclaimed—had lost his taste for brown beer. They remembered legends and old wives' tales about enchanted fishes who promised happiness: the tale of the talking flounder, who fulfilled a fisherman's greedy wife's every wish, all except the very last. The gentlemen became more and more fond of one another. How delightful that Rist should please to invite his friend Zesen to be his guest soon in Wedel. (I heard Buchner praising the absent Schottel's industriously compiled collection of words.) In a small bowl, the merchant Schlegel collected copper and silver coins to show the company's gratitude to the maids; and everyone, even the pious Gerhardt, gave something. When old Weckherlin, wishing, after and in spite of all that had happened, to do the landlady honor, bade her in courtly phrases leave the window and sit down at the table, we saw that Libuschka was wrapped in her horse blanket as though summer gave her the shivers. She did not hear him. She stood there absently, with rounded shoulders. Someone suggested that her thoughts were running after Stoffel.

Then there was talk of him and his green doublet. Since the poets were given to similes, the solitary young pike was likened to Gelnhausen and then allotted to his sponsor Harsdörffer. Several confided plans. It wasn't only the publishers—Mülbe and Endter in the lead—who wanted to get a few books out of the peace; the authors, too, had peace pageants or plays in the process of being written or rattling merrily around in their heads. Birken was planning an allegory in many parts for production in Nuremberg. Rist was intending to follow up his "Germany Yearning for Peace" with a "Germany Jubilant over the Peace." Harsdörffer felt sure that the court in Wolfenbüttel would welcome texts for ballets and operas. (Would Schütz be inclined to contribute great music?)

Still the landlady was showing her narrow back, humped under her blanket. But after Buchner had given it a try, not even Dach succeeded in persuading Libuschka or Courage or the obscurely begotten daughter of the Bohemian Count Thurn—or whoever else she might be—to join the poets at the long table. It was not until one of the maids (Elsabe?) spouted news while serving the last of the fried fish—it seemed that a troop of gypsies had camped on the Klatenberg and the Ems Gate had been locked—that I saw Libuschka start and prick up her ears. But when, in his farewell to all, Simon Dach gave thanks to the landlady, her thoughts were again elsewhere.

He stood smiling, surveyed the long table,

saw the bare fishbones heaped up between head and tail, and held the rolled and now sealed manifesto in his left hand. At the start of his speech there was something of a lump in his throat. But then, when he had devoted sufficient hard-found melancholy words to leave-taking, to the necessity of parting, and to the enduring ties of friendship, he spoke casually, freed from a burden, almost as though wishing to belittle the importance of the meeting, to patter away its weight. It cheered him, he said, to see that Greflinger's fish had made them all honest again. Whether the whole affair should be repeated at some auspicious time, he did not, or not yet, know, eagerly as he was being urged to set a place and time. Yes, he reflected, there had been vexations. Almost too many to count. But all in all the effort had proved worthwhile. After this, none of them would feel quite so isolated. And anyone who at home might feel constrained by narrow-mindedness, overwhelmed by new misery, deceived by false glitter, and in danger of losing the fatherland, was advised to remember the unscathed thistle at the Bridge Tavern hard by Telgte's Ems Gate, where the language had given promise of scope, supplied glitter, taken the place of the fatherland, and yielded names for all the misery of this world. No prince could equal them. Their riches could not be bought or sold. And even if they should be stoned and buried in hatred, a hand with a pen would rise out of the stone pile. They alone had the power to preserve for all time whatever truly deserved the name of German: "For, my dear and esteemed friends, brief as may be the time granted us to remain on earth, each one of our rhymes, provided our spirit has fashioned it from life, will mingle with eternity. . . ."

Then, cutting into Dach's speech, which soared to incorporate the assembled poets into eternity, cutting into his sentence about immortal poesy (during which he lifted up the rolled appeal for peace and likewise dedicated it to immortality), came the landlady's word from the window, not uttered loudly but sharpened to a cry: "Fire!"

Then the maids came running in with their screams. And only then—Simon Dach was still standing as though wanting in spite of it all to complete his speech—did we all smell smoke.

23

From the rear gable, whose damaged thatched roof frayed down over the windows of the great hall, the smolder had eaten into the drafty attic, where, drawing breath, it seized upon bales of straw, straw spread out for sleeping, litter, bundles of fagots, and forgotten lumber, burst into running flames that leapt up to the rafters, pierced the thatched roof on both sides, consumed the floorboards, tumbled with burning joists and planks into the great hall, invaded the front gable, and raced down the attic stairs and through the hallways, attacking the hastily evacuated open-doored rooms, so that sheaves of flame soon burst into the open from all the bedroom windows and, rising skyward at one with the flaming roof, gave the conflagration ultimate beauty.

That was how I saw it: the overwrought Zesen, the diabolical Gryf, all saw it differently—all those who had barely managed to escape into the courtyard with their luggage and had previously seen Glogau, Wittenberg, or Magdeburg in flames. No bolt held firm. From the vestibule, the blaze burst into the taproom, the kitchen, the landlady's alcove, and the remaining downstairs rooms. The Bridge Tavern had no other guest than fire; the lime trees planted on the weather side burned like torches. Despite the absence of wind, sparks flew. Greflinger had barely time, with the help of Lauremberg and Moscherosch, to lead the horses across the courtyard, push the remaining covered wagons into the outer gateway, and harness the terrified beasts; then the stable went up in flames. Lauremberg was kicked by a black horse, and from then on he limped on his right side. No one heard his lamentations. All were concerned with themselves. I alone saw the three maids load one mule with bundles and cooking pots. On the other mule sat Libuschka, her back to the fire, but still wrapped in her horse blanket, as calm as if nothing had happened, the dogs whimpering at her feet.

Birken lamented because his industriously filled journal had been left in the attic with the young men's luggage. The publisher Endter deplored the loss of a stack of books he had been planning to sell in Brunswick. The manifesto! cried Rist. Where? Who? Dach stood empty-handed. The German poets' appeal for peace had been forgotten among the fish-bones on the long table. In defiance of all reason, Logau wanted to run back into the taproom: to save the screed! Czepko had to hold him. And so, what would in any case not have been heard, remained unsaid.

When the roof of the Bridge Tavern collapsed and spark-spewing beams tumbled into the courtyard with chunks of thatch, the assembled poets and publishers gathered up their luggage and fled to the covered wagons. Schneuber looked after Lauremberg. Harsdörffer helped old Weckherlin. Gryphius and Zesen, who were still standing there enthralled by the fire, had to be called and shoved, and the praying Paul Gerhardt had to be wrenched out of his devotions.

Off to one side, Marthe Elsabe Marie prodded the pack mule and Libuschka's mount. The maid Marie told the student Scheffler that they were going to the Klatenberg. It almost looked as though the future Silesius were going with them to the gypsies. He leapt from the wagon, and Marie fobbed him off with a Catholic chain to which was attached the Telgte Madonna, stamped in silver. Without a word or gesture or backward glance, Libuschka rode off with her maids in the direction of the Outer Ems. The tavern dogs—four in number, as we now could see—followed them.

But the poets wanted to get home. In three covered wagons they arrived unharmed in Osnabrück, where they separated. Singly or in groups, as they had come, they started on the return journey. Lauremberg recovered from the horse's kick at Rist's parsonage. As far as Berlin, Gerhardt traveled with Dach and Albert. Without incurring serious danger, the Silesians reached home. Undeterred by the detour, the Nurembergers stopped off at Wolfenbüttel to report on the meeting. Buchner stopped in Köthen. Once again Weckherlin took ship in Bremen. Greflinger went to Hamburg, where he was planning to settle down. And Moscherosch? And Zesen?

None of us got lost. We all arrived. But during that century no one assembled us again in Telgte or anywhere else. I know how much further meetings would have meant to us. I know who I was then. I know even more. But who set the Bridge Tavern on fire I don't know, I don't know . . .

Afterword

Grass sets his meeting in Telgte, in Westphalia, in May of 1647. The negotiations leading up to the treaties of Westphalia, which brought the Thirty Years' War to an end, were well under way. In England the Civil War had reached its most critical phase; Cromwell had by now realized that there could be no accommodation with the king. "Old Weckherlin" (not so old by present-day standards—he was only sixty-three) in London was busier than he had ever been in his life as secretary of the Committee of Both Kingdoms (a sort of Anglo-Scottish war cabinet): not too busy to prepare a collected edition of his German poetry, which was published at Amsterdam the following year, but much too busy to take ship to Bremen in order to attend a meeting of German poets—he had too many meetings already. In America the four colonies of Massachusetts, Connecticut, New Haven, and Plymouth were maintaining their recently formed, uneasy confederation. In Germany everyone—the various German powers, the Swedes, the French—was jockeying for position and making secret deals about the transfer of German territory. Only England was no longer in a position to pursue the Stewart dynastic aim—the restitution of the Palatinate. On the surface the great division between Catholic and Protestant determined the confrontations, but vested interests of all kinds undermined this simple pattern, as indeed they had all along. The negotiations were held at the two cities of Osnabrück and Münster, thirty miles apart, one uneasily Protestant, the other firmly Catholic; emissaries posted hastily back and forth between the two. And between the two Grass situates his German poets, who had hoped to find accommodation at Oesede, close to Osnabrück, but who then had to settle for Telgte, close to Münster, a place of pilgrimage, whose miracle-working Madonna plays a part in the story and still draws thousands to the town. There they meet and feel themselves to represent German intellectual and literary life; in a fragmented and exhausted Germany, a rallying point for men of good will; a third force. To this end Grass brings them together in a meeting that never took place, that never could have taken place; indeed, it can be shown that none of the participants could have been in that place at that time—like Weckherlin.

Grass dedicates his book to Hans Werner Richter, and in the opening paragraph he makes it plain that he senses a parallel between events in 1647 and 1947. In 1947 Hans Werner Richter had gathered a number of German writers around him and formed a loose association of authors, critics, and publishers which provided a forum for reading and discussing new work. It met every year until 1967 and during those twenty years exerted a considerable influence on literature in West Germany. Grass himself first attended in 1955, and he was awarded the Prize of the Group 47 (as it came to be called) in 1958 for *The Tin Drum*. In his new book he has turned a kind of backward somersault and projected the twentieth-century group back into the seventeenth; he has put the question: What could we have done if we had been alive then? (In much the same way he has tried, in a more recent book, to envisage what he himself would have been like if he had been born ten years earlier and had thus been twenty-eight in 1945 instead of eighteen, with enlightening results; these imaginative gymnastics are more than just parlor tricks.)

German readers were quick to see the parallels, and critics looked eagerly for portraits (especially of themselves) as though Grass had written a *roman à clef*—but that is not the way the book works. There are some correspondences in detail between the two groups—readings of unpublished work, immediate criticism and comment to which the reader may not reply, the special seat in which the reader sits (known in the Group 47 as the "electric chair"), the presence of publishers and professors, and so on—enough to make it clear that a parallel is intended, but no more.

The parallel in the general situation of the two groups is clear. In 1647 the negotiations for peace after the most destructive war Germany had ever known were taking their mysterious and largely uncomprehended course; in 1947 negotiations for a peace treaty were being halfheartedly pursued and fronts were developing over the heads of the baffled and exhausted Germans after the most destructive war Germany has ever known. In an atmosphere of incomprehension and frustration people take recourse to art as something that can transcend political divisions. Grass's dust-jacket design (drawn, as always, by himself), the hand with the frail quill pen emerging from a pile of rubble, points in the same direction; it is perhaps inspired by a baroque emblem showing a standard bearing an uplifted hand with a motto enjoining unity and confidence. In a similar spirit, Hugo von Hofmannsthal spoke in 1927 of literature as the intellectual living space of the nation.

In 1647 Germany was divided between Catholics and Protestants; in 1947 the division between the three Western zones of occupation on the one hand and the Soviet zone on the other was hardening; it later gave rise to the divided Germany we now know. The writers who came together in 1947 were from the Western zones (where an intellectual journal planned by Hans Werner Richter had been banned by American censorship); they were as critical of developments in the capitalist West as of those in the socialist East, and tried to maintain what in 1647 would have been called an "irenic" position. It is not for nothing that the poets Grass assembles in Telgte continually refer to men who represented what we would call now an "ecumenical" stand transcending denominational divisions. And just as in 1947 the group was firmly rooted in the West and despite all criticism in detail was oriented to Western thinking, so the poets in Telgte are firmly Protestant— indeed, Lutheran—in their thinking. German literature in 1647 was in fact almost exclusively Lutheran; the language of literature was the language of Luther's Bible. The purification of the German language in 1647 meant the elimination of foreign words (mostly Latin and French); in 1947 it meant the avoidance of Nazi terminology and Nazi-tainted concepts: in both cases the creation of a new idiom.

The meeting in Telgte was not a success; the voice of the third force went unheard because circumstances—fire and chance—were too strong. So why lay this account of a failure at the feet of a respected colleague? Because he had achieved what Simon Dach and his friends could not: his achievement is seen afresh in the light of what might have been attempted three hundred years before but could not possibly have succeeded. The pen rising triumphant out of the rubble of the destroyed cities was Richter's achievement, not Dach's.

LEONARD FORSTER

Dramatis Personae

HEINRICH ALBERT (1604–1651): Composer and poet. He and SIMON DACH were the leading figures of the Königsberg circle of poets. He set his friends' verses to music in four parts and published them together with his settings.

JAKOB BALDE (1604–1668): Jesuit Latin poet with a European reputation, admired by ANDREAS GRYPHIUS, who translated some of his lyric poems.

CORNELIUS BECKER (1561–1604): The author of metrical psalms for church use, set to familiar German tunes, a Lutheran counter to the German version of the Calvinist Huguenot metrical psalter by AMBROSIUS LOBWASSER, which was set to French tunes.

MATHIAS BERNEGGER (1582–1640): Professor in Strasbourg and an important figure in the intellectual life of the city. Himself a Protestant refugee from Austria, he stood for a liberal humanism transcending denominational barriers and maintained an extensive and influential correspondence with scholars in other countries.

SIEGMUND VON BIRKEN (1620–1681): A Protestant refugee from Bohemia brought up in Nuremberg, where he became a leading figure in the local literary society, the PEGNITZ SHEPHERDS, and an extremely prolific writer. Contemporary portraits confirm his handsome face and curly hair, mentioned by Grass.

GEORG BLUM (d. 1648): A Prussian official and friend of DACH, ALBERT, and ROBERTHIN.

JAKOB BÖHME (1575–1624): A mystical shoemaker, often called *Philosophus teutonicus,* who sought to restore into a harmony the dualities of which men were aware. His writings were extremely influential, especially among his fellow Silesians, notably ABRAHAM VON FRANCKENBERG, JOHANN SCHEFFLER, and DANIEL VON CZEPKO, but also in England and America, where they influenced George Fox and the early Quakers.

AUGUST BUCHNER (1591–1661): A friend of MARTIN OPITZ and professor of poetry at Wittenberg. His views on the theory and practice of poetry were greatly respected during his lifetime, though they did not appear in print until after his death, compiled from students' lecture notes. His advocacy of dactyls and anapests went beyond Opitz's restriction of German verse to iambics and trochees and extended the resources of German poetry considerably, especially in the hands of HARSDÖRFFER and BIRKEN; among his pupils were KLAJ, ZESEN, and GERHARDT. The rivalry between Buchner and SCHOTTEL, who also was one of his pupils, seems to have been invented by Grass.

DANIEL VON CZEPKO UND REIGERSFELD (1591–1661): Silesian religious poet. He studied in Strasbourg under BERNEGGER and became a lawyer. In 1647 he was living on his estates as a country gentleman. His works circulated mainly in manuscript; his mystical epigrams were an important source of inspiration for JOHANN SCHEFFLER.

SIMON DACH (1605–1659): Professor of poetry in Königsberg and the most important figure in the Königsberg circle of poets (see also ALBERT, BLUM, ROBERTHIN) following OPITZ. Much of his lyric poetry appeared in the musical publications of his friend ALBERT, but more of it consisted of occasional pieces written to order. His great poem on the destruction of the cucumber bower, referred to by Grass, was not published until 1936. The poem "Annie of Tharaw," translated by Longfellow and referred to by Grass, is now generally thought to be by ALBERT.

LUDWIG ELZEVIHR [LODEWIJK ELSEVIER] (1604–1670): A member of the important Dutch publishing dynasty of Elsevier or Elzevir, the namesake and grandson of the founder of the firm. He established the Amsterdam branch and published many of the works of PHILIPP VON ZESEN.

WOLFGANG ENDTER (1593–1659): An important publisher in Nuremberg, specializing in Lutheran devotional literature and the works of members of the PEGNITZ SHEPHERDS (especially HARSDÖRFFER and KLAJ). He did in fact publish the work by JOHANN RIST on the conclusion of peace, referred to by Grass.

ALEXANDER ERSKEIN (1598–1656): Swedish general of German-Scottish antecedents. Despite his cavalier treatment of the poets in this book, he was in fact a member of the FRUIT-BEARING SOCIETY, though there is no other evidence of his interest in literature.

PAUL FLEMING (1609–1640): One of the major figures in German seventeenth-century literature. He took part in an embassy from the Duke of Holstein-Gottorp to Russia and Persia, in the course of which he spent a year in Reval and became engaged to Elsabe Niehus, the daughter of a city councilor. On his return he found she had married another, and he became engaged to her sister Anna. He went to Leiden to complete his medical studies but died suddenly before he could practice. His poetry, mainly lyrical, was highly thought of at the time, and still is. Some of his hymns have passed into church use in Germany, and a few in England as well.

ABRAHAM VON FRANCKENBERG (1593–1652): Silesian nobleman and mystical writer influenced by JAKOB BÖHME, whose biography he wrote. He was a friend of CZEPKO and SCHEFFLER and lived for a time in Danzig.

GIOVANNI GABRIELI (d. 1613): Venetian composer who had many contacts with Germany, the teacher of HEINRICH SCHÜTZ.

CHRISTOFFEL GELNHAUSEN: See GRIMMELSHAUSEN.

PAUL GERHARDT (1607–1676): As an orthodox Lutheran pastor under a Calvinist prince, he experienced in his own person the dissensions among Protestants. He is the greatest German hymn-writer; twenty-seven of his hymns have been translated into English, and sixteen of them are in English church use, including "I know that my Redeemer liveth" and "O sacred Head, surrounded"; the original of "Now all the woods are sleeping," referred to by Grass, was not actually in print in 1647.

GEORG GREFLINGER (c. 1620–1667): After a checkered career, he settled down in Hamburg in 1646 as a notary public and produced many translations. From 1665 on he published the *Nordischer Mercurius,* one of the best newspapers of the century.

209

JOHANN JAKOB CHRISTOFFEL VON GRIMMELSHAUSEN (1621–1676): Appears here under the name of Christoffel Gelnhausen (after his birthplace, Gelnhausen, in Hesse). He wrote the picaresque and largely autobiographical novel *Simplicissimus* (1668), which is one of the great works of German literature. It deals with the author's variegated career in the Thirty Years' War and was continued and complemented in a number of further writings, which together make up a wide-ranging cycle. Grass's Gelnhausen has many traits in common with Simplicissimus, whose female counterpart is the heroine of one of these novels, with the name of Courasche; she appears in her own person in Grass's book as Libuschka. There are English translations of *Simplicissimus* by A. T. S. Goodrick (1912) and George Schulz-Behrendt (1965), of *Courasche* by Walter Wallich (1965) and Hans Speier (1964).

HUGO GROTIUS (1583–1645): Dutch humanist, diplomat, and international lawyer, universally respected in his day as a scholar and still a key figure in legal history. He was important in the irenic movement in the seventeenth century and was in contact with OPITZ, BERNEGGER, and LINGELSHEIM.

ANDREAS GRYPHIUS (1616–1664): With OPITZ, FLEMING, SCHEFFLER, and GRIMMELSHAUSEN, a major figure in German seventeenth-century literature, both as a lyric poet and as a dramatist. Grass incorporated a memorable scene between the young Gryphius and the middle-aged Opitz in *The Flounder*. Some of Gryphius's religious poems have been translated for English church use. Besides his literary activity, which began early, he was a scholarly polymath who refused chairs at Uppsala and Heidelberg in order to enter the public service in Silesia.

GIAMBATTISTA GUARINI (1538–1612): Italian court poet. He wrote the classic pastoral play *Il pastor fido*

(1580), which had a European vogue and was translated into German by HOFMANNSWALDAU. Many of his poems were set to music.

GEORG PHILIPP HARSDÖRFFER (1607–1658): The central figure of literary life in seventeenth-century Nuremberg. Together with JOHANN KLAJ he founded the literary society of the PEGNITZ SHEPHERDS, to which BIRKEN also belonged, in 1644. He studied at Strasbourg under BERNEGGER and eagerly adopted the metrical theories of BUCHNER. Besides being active in public life as a councilor of the city-state of Nuremberg, he was a prolific writer and a popularizer of contemporary science, philosophy, and literature.

CHRISTIAN HOFMANN VON HOFMANNSWALDAU (1616–1679): Silesian nobleman and man of affairs. He wrote technically accomplished poetry comparable to that of the Restoration poets in England, but whereas they really were rakes, he really was not. His poems circulated widely in manuscript and set the tone for poetic production in Germany throughout the second half of the century, as OPITZ's had for the first half. They were not collected until after his death.

JOHANN KLAJ (1616–1656): With HARSDÖRFFER, the moving spirit of the Nuremberg literary society of the PEGNITZ SHEPHERDS.

BERNHARD KNIPPERDOLLING (d. 1536): In 1534 a revolutionary group of Anabaptists led by Bernd Rottmann, Jan Beuckelson van Leiden, and Bernhard Knipperdolling took over the city of Münster and established a theocratic state. They abolished Sundays and holy days, instituted love feasts, practiced polygamy, executed hostile citizens, and did away with all books except the Bible.

JOHANN LAUREMBERG (1590–1658): Professor of poetry at Rostock, his native town, later professor of mathematics at Sorø in Denmark. He wrote satires in Low German expressing a sturdy conservatism, one of which he reads in this book. They were, however, not actually in print at the time and did not appear until 1652.

LIBUSCHKA: See GRIMMELSHAUSEN.

GEORG MICHAEL LINGELSHEIM (1556–1636): Humanist and statesman in the service of the Palatinate, the principal figure of a literary circle in Heidelberg, in the early years of the century, to which ZINCGREF and the young OPITZ belonged. He maintained an extensive irenic and scholarly correspondence, especially with MATHIAS BERNEGGER.

AMBROSIUS LOBWASSER (1515–1585): In 1573 he translated the Huguenot metrical psalms (by Clément Marot and Théodore de Bèze) into German, retaining the original meters. This translation, though Calvinist (see also BECKER), was influential in Lutheran circles and continued in use until the eighteenth century.

FRIEDRICH VON LOGAU (1604–1655): Silesian nobleman and official, author of epigrams, two hundred of which appeared in 1638; the final collection, which appeared in 1653, comprised three thousand. They embody social and political satire in pregnant form.

LUDWIG, PRINCE OF ANHALT-KÖTHEN (1579–1650): Head of the FRUIT-BEARING SOCIETY.

GIAMBATTISTA MARINO (1569–1625): Italian poet in the high baroque style, greatly admired by HOFMANNSWALDAU. His poems were often set to music.

CLAUDIO MONTEVERDI (1567–1643): Italian composer who wrote the first operatic masterpiece, *Orfeo* (1607).

212

JOHANN MICHAEL MOSCHEROSCH (1601–1669): Novelist and satirist of remote Spanish (apparently Marrano) antecedents, whose descriptions of life at the time of the Thirty Years' War (1642) were inspired by the *Sueños* (*Dreams*) of the Spanish author Francisco de Quevedo. Grass's allusions to his presumed Jewishness refer to his Marrano ancestry.

JOHANN PHILIPP MÜLBE (1625–1667): Strasbourg publisher who brought out the works of MOSCHEROSCH and SCHNEUBER, among others.

JOHANN NAUMANN (1627–1668): Hamburg publisher who issued works by RIST and ZESEN, but not, as Grass seems to imply, by MOSCHEROSCH.

GEORG NEUMARK (1621–1681): He studied law in Königsberg, where he had contacts with DACH and other members of his circle. By 1647 he had only published one pastoral novel. He later became librarian and archivist in Weimar and kept the archives of the FRUIT-BEARING SOCIETY.

MARTIN OPITZ (1597–1639): By his reform of versification, reducing metrics to an easily grasped regular alternation of stressed and unstressed syllables (iambics and trochaics), he brought German poetry into line with what was being written elsewhere in Europe. He himself provided specimen models of the most important literary genres, either by translation or by original composition. Throughout the century he was regarded as the "father of German poetry." See also GRYPHIUS.

OTTAVIO RINUCCINI (1552–1621): Italian poet and author of libretti for the first operas, including the *Arianna* (1608), of MONTEVERDI. OPITZ translated his libretto *Dafne* for music by Heinrich Schütz (now lost).

JOHANN RIST (1607–1667): A learned country parson, author of works of popular science and theology. He was a faithful follower of OPITZ in his numerous works of poetry. Seventeen of his religious poems have been translated into English for church use, including "Eternity, thou word of fear." He founded the ORDER OF ELBE SWANS in 1658. His feud with ZESEN, referred to by Grass, did not break out until 1648, though their relations were strained before that.

ROBERT ROBERTHIN (1600–1648): Prussian official, a friend of DACH and ALBERT and a pupil of BERNEGGER.

JESAIAS ROMPLER VON LÖWENHALT (1628–1658): Together with SCHNEUBER, he founded the UPRIGHT SOCIETY OF THE PINE TREE in Strasbourg in 1633.

JOHANN SCHEFFLER (1630–1677): Silesian medical student in contact with the mystical circle around ABRAHAM VON FRANCKENBERG and CZEPKO. He was converted to Catholicism in 1652 and assumed the name of Angelus Silesius; he took orders in 1661 and became the moving spirit of the Counter-Reformation in Silesia. By virtue of his religious pastoral poems and his mystical epigrams, many written before his conversion, he is one of the great names in German literature. Some thirty of his poems have been translated for English church use, including "O Love who formedst me to wear." At the time of the meeting at Telgte he was in fact studying medicine in Italy. There is an English translation of his epigrams by J. E. C. Flitch (1932).

JOHANN MATHIAS SCHNEUBER (1614–1665): Professor of poetry in Strasbourg, member of the PINE TREE SOCIETY and a friend of ROMPLER VON LÖWENHALT and MOSCHEROSCH.

JUSTUS GEORG SCHOTTEL (1612–1676): The leading linguistic theorist of seventeenth-century Germany;

his work on normative and systematic linguistics of the German language is still important. He was an official of the court of Brunswick-Wolfenbüttel for most of his life. His rivalry with BUCHNER seems to have been invented by Grass.

HEINRICH SCHÜTZ (1585–1672): One of the greatest precursors of Bach; he composed mainly religious music but also the earliest German opera, *Dafne,* to a text by OPITZ after RINUCCINI. The score is lost.

FRIEDRICH SPEE VON LANGENFELD (1591-1635): A Jesuit, the first important writer of sacred poetry in Catholic Germany in the vernacular after the Reformation. Several of his religious poems have passed into English church use. He published anonymously an attack on witch hunting to which Grass refers, based on his experience as chaplain in Würzburg. This was the only work of his to appear in his lifetime.

TORQUATO TASSO (1544–1595): Italian lyric and epic poet. The combat between Tancredi and Clorinda from the twelfth book of his epic *Gerusalemme liberata* (1576) was frequently set to music.

ANDREAS TSCHERNING (1611–1659): Professor of poetry in Rostock and a pupil and friend of BUCHNER.

GEORG RUDOLF WECKHERLIN (1584–1653): Lyric poet and civil servant. From 1620 on he lived and worked in London and was Milton's predecessor as Latin secretary under the Commonwealth. His residence in London put him out of touch with developments in Germany, but before that he was a pioneer of baroque poetry in Germany before OPITZ and continued to be respected later, especially by South German opponents of Opitz like ROMPLER and his PINE TREE SOCIETY.

PHILIPP VON ZESEN (1619–1689): Poet and novelist who lived largely by his pen at Amsterdam (one of the first German authors to do so). He founded a literary society, the GERMAN-MINDED ASSOCIATION, in Hamburg in 1642. He followed the metrical theories of BUCHNER, whose pupil he was, and he was in touch with the Nuremberg group, especially HARSDÖRFFER. His feud with RIST is referred to by Grass.

JULIUS WILHELM ZINCGREF (1591–1635): Palatine diplomat and official, and a prominent member of the Heidelberg circle around LINGELSHEIM. He published the first collected volume of poetry by OPITZ in Strasbourg in 1624 and an influential collection of proverbs and apothegms in 1626.

Literary Societies

Grass mentions six. These societies were founded for the cultivation and purification of the German language after the model of the Italian academies, especially the Accademia della Crusca (Florence 1582). The main aims of all were similar: the cultivation of the German language, the worship of God, and the pursuit of virtue; in other words, they were social and moral as well as linguistic and literary. Many literary men belonged to more than one; this circumstance, as well as the similarity of aims, meant that the rivalry which Grass assumes to have existed was not important though there were differences of policy and emphasis. The Pegnitz Shepherds, for instance, admitted women on an equal footing with men; the Fruit-bearing Society discriminated against the clergy and in favor of the nobility; the Pine Tree resisted the literary hegemony of Silesia; and so on. These societies represented attempts at organizing the literary world—producers and consumers and patrons—which continued despite the vicissitudes of the Thirty Years' War; they also sponsored publications, either directly or indirectly. All the societies dealt with here were Protestant, though the Pegnitz Shepherds admitted a few Catholics. All aimed at producing grammars, dictionaries, manuals of poetics, and translations, and at providing models of the various literary genres, though not all actually did so. In all societies the members received special names, emblems, and insignia. Business was conducted mainly by correspondence; no general meeting of any society is recorded. If there had been one, it would probably have been very much like the meeting at Telgte, though doubtless more formal.

GERMAN-MINDED ASSOCIATION (*Deutschgesinnte Genossenschaft*): Founded by ZESEN in 1642, with seat at first in Hamburg, later in Amsterdam. Members included BIRKEN, HARSDÖRFFER, KLAJ, MOSCHEROSCH, and ROMPLER; many were of noble birth.

ORDER OF ELBE SWANS (*Elbschwanenorden*): Founded by RIST in 1658, apparently as a subsidiary of the FRUIT-BEARING SOCIETY.

FRUIT-BEARING SOCIETY (*Fruchtbringende Gesellschaft, Palmenorden*): The first and most prestigious of the literary societies, founded in 1617 under the presidency of Prince Ludwig of Anhalt-Köthen, who was already a member of the Accademia della Crusca. By 1652 it had 527 members, most of whom were of noble birth and relatively few of whom were greatly concerned with literature. Nonetheless the influence of the society was important, thanks to the consistent critical work put in by its first president; its tendency was irenic. Among its members were BIRKEN, BUCHNER, GRYPHIUS, HARSDÖRFFER, LOGAU, MOSCHEROSCH, OPITZ, SCHOTTEL, RIST, and ZESEN, though not by any means all of them at the time Grass's story takes place.

PEGNITZ SHEPHERDS (*Pegnitzschäfer, Blumenorden*): Founded by HARSDÖRFFER and KLAJ in Nuremberg in 1644, partly inspired by Sir Philip Sidney's *Arcadia*. Few members were of noble birth, but many were from the patriciate of the cities. Women were admitted as members (though very few). HARSDÖRFFER, the first president, had admitted only fourteen members by 1658; his successor BIRKEN admitted many more.

CUCUMBER LODGE (*Kürbishütte*): Not a literary society in the then accepted sense, with a constitution, officers, insignia, etc., but an informal group of friends meeting at intervals, usually in HEINRICH ALBERT's garden in Königsberg in a bower overgrown with cucumbers (cp. Isaiah I:8), where they used to sing their own songs set to music by him. Among the members were DACH, ALBERT, BLUME, and ROBERTHIN; OPITZ once paid them a visit.

UPRIGHT SOCIETY OF THE PINE TREE (*Aufrichtige Tannengesellschaft*): Founded in Strasbourg in 1633 by ROMPLER, as a rallying point for South German opponents of OPITZ. MOSCHEROSCH and WECKHERLIN may have been members. SCHNEUBER was a cofounder.

Further information will be found in Henry and Mary Garland, *The Oxford Companion to German Literature*, Clarendon Press, 1976, and, since the seventeenth century was the great period of hymnwriting and most of our poets wrote hymns, in John Julian, *A Dictionary of Hymnology*, 2nd edition, London, 1892, reprinted New York, 1957. All the poets appearing in Grass's book are represented in the original and in verse translation in George C. Schoolfield, *The German Lyric of the Baroque in English Translation* (University of North Carolina Studies in the Germanic Languages and Literature, No. 29, Chapel Hill, N.C., 1961), with a very useful introduction on German seventeenth-century lyric poetry in general.